The 8-Week Bar Exam Study Schedule

A Step-by-Step Daily Plan to Cover Every Topic and Pass the Bar

Caine Audrey Lehnert

Disclaimer

This publication is intended for educational and informational purposes only. It does not constitute legal advice, professional counsel, or a guarantee of exam results.

While every effort has been made to ensure the accuracy and reliability of the content, including the practice questions and explanations, the author and publisher make no representations or warranties regarding the completeness, correctness, or current applicability of the material. The questions in this book are original creations designed to reflect the style and substance of standardized legal examinations but are not official questions from any bar exam authority.

Use of the practice questions is at the reader's discretion. Performance on these questions should not be interpreted as a predictor of performance on any official bar examination. Exam content, structure, and standards may vary by jurisdiction and change over time. Readers are responsible for confirming current exam formats and rules with the appropriate licensing authority.

All names, characters, case facts, and scenarios used in the questions are entirely fictional and created solely for illustrative purposes. Any resemblance to actual persons, living or dead, or to real events, legal cases, or organizations is purely coincidental.

By using this book, readers agree that the author and publisher shall not be held liable for any direct or indirect loss, consequence, or damage resulting from the use or reliance on this material. Always seek qualified legal or academic support for individualized guidance.

Isohan Publishing

ISBN: 978-1-923370-44-9

Table of Contents

Introduction: Your 8-Week Path to Passing the Bar 1

Part 1: Laying the Foundation (Pre-Week 1) 9

Chapter 1: Know Your Enemy - Understanding Your Bar Exam 10

Chapter 2: Assembling Your Arsenal - Resources and Study Environment 17

Chapter 3: The Starting Line - Diagnostic Assessment and Goal Setting 23

Chapter 4: Preparing for the Sprint - Logistics and Well-being 30

Part 2: The 8-Week Daily Breakdown 37

Chapter 5: Week 1 - Building the Base 38

Chapter 6: Week 2 - Expanding Core Knowledge 46

Chapter 7: Week 3 - Integrating Concepts 55

Chapter 8: Week 4 - Midpoint Check-in & MEE Subjects 63

Chapter 9: Week 5 - Ramping Up Practice 73

Chapter 10: Week 6 - Simulation and Refinement 81

Chapter 11: Week 7 - Peak Practice & Weak Area Attack 88

Chapter 12: Week 8 - Final Polish and Exam Readiness 95

Part 3: Strategy, Execution, and Beyond 102

Chapter 13: Mastering the Components - Advanced Techniques 103

Chapter 14: Learning from Practice - Analyzing Performance 111

Chapter 15: The Final Week - Countdown to Exam Day 118

Chapter 16: Conquering the Exam Days 125

Part 4: Practice Questions 131

Practice Exam 1 132

Practice Exam 2 160

Conclusion: Crossing the Finish Line 189

References 197

Introduction: Your 8-Week Path to Passing the Bar

So, you're facing the bar exam. It looms large, doesn't it? A big, often frightening, hurdle standing between you and the title "Attorney at Law." You've likely heard the stories, felt the pressure, and maybe even experienced the sheer bewilderment of figuring out *how* exactly one prepares for this monster of an assessment. Many people search desperately online, typing things like "pass the bar fast" or "bar exam study schedule," hoping for a magic bullet. Well, this book isn't magic—it's a plan. A very specific, demanding, eight-week plan designed to guide you through the necessary material and practice, day by day. It's built on the idea that intense, structured effort over a defined period can be remarkably effective, especially when compared to months of unfocused, anxiety-ridden "studying." If you're looking for a shortcut that involves no work, this isn't it. But if you're looking for a clear path that requires your dedication, keep reading.

Why an 8-Week Schedule?

Why cram it into eight weeks? Couldn't you just spread it out over six months? You certainly could—and many people do. Commercial bar prep courses often run for ten to twelve weeks.[1] However, there's a point of diminishing returns. Stretching studying out too long can lead to burnout, forgetting material learned early on, and a persistent, low-grade anxiety that drains your energy. Think about it—sustaining peak mental effort for half a year is extraordinarily difficult, maybe even impossible for most humans.

An eight-week schedule demands **intensity and focus**. It concentrates your efforts into a period short enough to maintain momentum but long enough (just barely!) to cover the required ground. It forces you to be efficient. There's little room for procrastination or unproductive wallowing in how "hard" it all is (which, let's be honest, it *is* hard—but wallowing doesn't get you points). This shorter timeframe necessitates a **highly structured approach**, which is exactly what this book provides. You won't waste precious time wondering *what* to study each day. The plan tells you. Your job is to execute it.

Consider **Alex**, who tried a six-month, self-designed study plan while working part-time. For the first two months, things seemed fine. He read outlines leisurely, did a few practice questions here and there. But by month four, he realized he barely remembered the details of Torts or Contracts he'd covered initially. His motivation waned. The finish line felt impossibly far away. He was studying *longer*, but not necessarily *better*. An intense, eight-week schedule, while demanding upfront, forces constant engagement and review, reducing the chance of knowledge fading away before exam day. It's a sprint, not a meandering walk in the park.

Who This Book Is For

This plan isn't necessarily for everyone, but it's specifically designed for certain situations:

1. **Self-Studiers:** If you're piecing together your own bar prep using various resources instead of enrolling in a full-service commercial course, you absolutely need structure. This book provides that framework, telling you what to study, when, and how much. It takes the guesswork out of organizing your time, which is often half the battle when studying alone.

2. **Retakers:** Facing the bar exam again is tough. Really tough. You might feel discouraged, frustrated, or convinced you're just "not smart enough" (which is almost certainly irrational nonsense). Often, the issue wasn't lack of intelligence; it was an ineffective study method, poor time management, or unaddressed weak areas. This structured 8-week plan forces a different approach. It emphasizes consistent practice across *all* subjects and skills, leaving no stone unturned. It helps break old, unproductive habits and provides a fresh, focused strategy. **Maria**, for example, failed her first attempt after following a standard course but skipping essay practice because it felt "too hard" and made her anxious. For her second attempt, using a rigorous daily schedule forced her to confront essay writing regularly, demystifying it and building competence through sheer, structured repetition. She didn't magically start *loving* essays, but she learned to *do* them effectively—and she passed.

3. **Time-Constrained Students:** Maybe you have significant work or family commitments that only allow for a dedicated eight-week window of intense study leave. Or perhaps you learn best under pressure, finding that shorter deadlines sharpen your focus. This plan maximizes efficiency within that compressed timeframe. It assumes you are treating these eight weeks as your primary focus, a full-time job (and then some).

If you're fresh out of law school with zero commitments and six months to kill, you *could* use a slower pace. But even then, the structure and intensity here might yield better results than a more relaxed approach.

The Philosophy Structure Discipline Active Learning and Adaptability

The approach underpinning this 8-week schedule rests on a few core ideas. Believing these ideas—or at least acting *as if* you believe them—will make following the plan much more effective.

- **Structure is Your Friend, Not Your Enemy:** Some people resist schedules, thinking they're too rigid. Nonsense. For a task like bar prep, structure is liberating. It frees your mind from the constant, energy-draining task of deciding *what* to do next. The schedule makes the decision; you just do the work. It ensures balance, preventing you from only studying your favorite subjects (a common mistake!) or neglecting critical skills like essay writing or the performance test.
- **Discipline is Simply Self-Management:** Discipline isn't about punishment or forcing yourself to do things you hate just because.[2] It's about making choices that align with your long-term goal (passing the bar) even when short-term discomfort arises (like tackling a difficult subject). Following this schedule is an act of disciplined self-management. It requires showing up, day after day, and doing the assigned tasks. You won't always *feel* like it. That's irrelevant. Your feelings don't dictate your actions unless you let them. Choose actions that serve your goal.
- **Active Learning Beats Passive Review:** Simply reading outlines or watching lectures is not enough. It creates an illusion of competence. True learning for the bar exam comes from *doing*—answering practice questions, writing out full essays, outlining performance tests, and actively grappling with the material. This schedule heavily emphasizes active learning tasks every single day. You will *produce* much more than you passively consume.
- **Adaptability Means Rational Adjustment, Not Catastrophizing:** Life happens. You might get sick for a day. An unavoidable commitment might pop up. The schedule *will* occasionally be disrupted. The key is how you respond. Do you throw your hands up and declare, "It's ruined! I'm hopelessly behind! I might as well give up!"? That's catastrophizing—an irrational response. Or do you

calmly assess the situation, figure out how to adjust the *next* day's plan (maybe shifting a task, slightly shortening another), and get back on track without demanding perfection? **Adaptability means accepting reality** (you missed a study block) **and making rational adjustments**, not demanding that reality conform to your rigid, perfect plan. This schedule is a template, a strong guide—not an inflexible dictator.

How to Use This Book and The Daily Plan

This book *is* the plan. Part 2 lays out the schedule week by week, day by day. Here's how to approach it:

1. **Read Part 1 First:** Don't just jump to Week 1, Day 1. The initial chapters help you understand your specific exam, gather resources, assess your starting point, and prepare your life—all necessary groundwork.

2. **Commit to the Structure:** The daily schedule provides blocks for substantive review, MBE practice, Essay/MPT practice, and review. Follow this structure. It's designed to mix learning modes and prevent burnout from doing one type of task for too long.

3. **Execute the Daily Tasks:** Each day specifies *what* subjects or skills to focus on and *what* types of activities to do (e.g., "Review Contracts Outline - Formation," "50 MBE Questions - Contracts," "Write 1 Contracts Essay - Timed"). Do them. Don't substitute easier tasks for harder ones just because you feel like it.

4. **Prioritize Active Tasks:** If you're short on time on a given day (which you shouldn't be, ideally—see Chapter 4!), prioritize the active tasks: practice questions, essays, MPTs. Passive review is easier to catch up on later.

5. **Use the Review Blocks Wisely:** The schedule includes time for reviewing incorrect answers. This is absolutely essential. Understanding *why* you got a question wrong is how you learn and improve. Don't skip this step.

6. **Embrace Flexibility Rationally:** As mentioned, life interferes. If you miss a few hours or even a day, **don't panic and don't quit**. Look at the schedule for the *next* day. Can you slightly adjust? Maybe do slightly fewer practice questions? Combine two short review sessions? The goal is consistent effort, not impossible perfection. Missing one block and getting right back on track the

next day is infinitely better than letting one disruption derail your entire process because you've told yourself you've failed.

7. **Track Your Progress:** Note your scores on practice sets. Keep a log of essay topics you've written. This helps you see improvement (which is motivating!) and identify persistent weak areas that need extra attention, perhaps by slightly adjusting the focus during scheduled review times.

Setting Realistic Expectations Effort Sacrifice and Mindset

Let's be brutally honest here—preparing for the bar exam in eight weeks is intense. It requires significant **effort** and **sacrifice**. Thinking otherwise is setting yourself up for disappointment and possibly quitting.

- **Effort:** Expect to work long hours. The schedule assumes roughly 8-10 hours of focused study per day, six days a week, with slightly lighter work or catch-up/review on the seventh day. This isn't passive clock-watching; it's engaged mental work. It will be tiring. It will be challenging. Sometimes, it will feel downright awful. Accept this as part of the process. Demanding that bar prep feel good or easy is an irrational belief that causes unnecessary distress.
- **Sacrifice:** For these eight weeks, bar study needs to be your top priority. This likely means sacrificing social events, hobbies, relaxation time, and perhaps even some sleep (though adequate sleep is actually quite important—we'll cover that). You need to communicate this clearly to family, friends, and employers. They need to understand that your availability will be extremely limited. Trying to maintain your normal life *while* layering this intense schedule on top is a recipe for failure and burnout. It requires temporarily putting other parts of your life on hold. It's unpleasant, yes, but temporary.
- **Mindset:** This is arguably the most overlooked aspect. You *will* face moments of doubt, anxiety, and frustration. You *will* get questions wrong. You *will* encounter topics that seem impossible to understand. How you *think* about these challenges drastically affects your ability to persevere.
    - **Challenge Catastrophic Thinking:** Instead of "I failed this MBE set, I'm going to fail the bar exam!", think: "Okay, I scored lower than I wanted on this set. Let me review the explanations carefully to see what I missed. This is an opportunity to learn."

- **Dispute Demands/Musts:** Instead of "I *must* understand Constitutional Law perfectly right now!", try: "I would *prefer* to understand Con Law easily, but it's a complex subject. I will keep working on it, do practice questions, and my understanding will improve over time. It doesn't *have* to be perfect today."

- **Practice Unconditional Self-Acceptance (USA):** Your worth as a person is *not* tied to passing the bar exam. Failing the bar exam would be highly inconvenient, disappointing, and frustrating—but it would not make *you* a failure as a human being. Accepting yourself, flaws and all, even if you struggle or fail, paradoxically makes it *easier* to put in the effort and take the risks needed to succeed. You perform better when your entire self-worth isn't riding on the outcome.

A Note on Your Specific Bar Exam UBE vs State Specific Components

This book uses the common components of the Uniform Bar Exam (UBE) as its primary framework—the Multistate Bar Examination (MBE), the Multistate Essay Examination (MEE), and the Multistate Performance Test (MPT). Most states use some or all of these components.

However, your specific jurisdiction might have variations:

- **Different Number of Essays/MPTs:** Some states use fewer MEEs or MPTs than the standard UBE.
- **State-Specific Subjects:** Many states add essays on state-specific laws (e.g., community property, state civil procedure).
- **State Multiple-Choice:** Some states have their own multiple-choice sections in addition to or instead of the MBE.

How to Adapt This Plan:

1. **Identify Your Exam's Components:** First, know exactly what your state tests. Go to your state bar examiners' website. Don't guess.
2. **Map Subjects:** Make a list of all the subjects tested on your exam (MBE, MEE, state-specific). Ensure your study materials cover everything.

3. **Adjust Essay/MPT Time:** If your state has fewer essays or MPTs, you might slightly reduce the *total* time allocated to those practice types *later* in the schedule (Weeks 5-8) and perhaps add more time for state-specific subjects or MBE practice. However, **do not skimp on fundamental essay/MPT skills practice early on**. The techniques are transferable.
4. **Incorporate State-Specific Material:** You MUST allocate time to learn and practice any state-specific subjects. You can substitute state-specific essay practice for some MEE practice slots in the schedule, especially in the later weeks. Treat state multiple-choice questions like MBE practice, incorporating them into those blocks. You might need to add an extra hour some days or use some weekend time specifically for state material if your state tests many unique subjects.

The core schedule—balancing substantive review, multiple-choice practice, and writing practice daily—remains the same. You just need to ensure the *content* you're plugging into those slots matches what *your* specific bar exam requires. Be rational and systematic about this mapping.

Moving Forward

So, there you have it. The premise, the philosophy, the structure, and the unvarnished reality of what this 8-week plan entails. It's not a magic wand, but it is a clear, actionable path. It demands work, focus, and a willingness to manage your own thinking—especially when things get tough.[3] If you're ready to commit to that process, then turn the page and let's start laying the foundation for your success. The next step is understanding exactly what you're up against by examining the specifics of your bar exam.

Key Takeaways from the Introduction

- An 8-week schedule offers intensity and focus, potentially combating burnout and forgetfulness associated with longer plans.

- This plan is particularly suited for self-studiers needing structure, retakers needing a fresh approach, and those with limited time.
- Success hinges on embracing structure, exercising disciplined self-management (doing the work feelings), prioritizing active learning (practice!), and adapting rationally (not catastrophizing) to disruptions.
- Use the book by following the daily structure, executing assigned tasks (especially active ones), reviewing mistakes thoroughly, and tracking progress.
- Expect intense effort and sacrifice; managing your mindset by challenging catastrophic thoughts and irrational demands ("musts") is essential for perseverance.
- Unconditional self-acceptance (separating your worth from the outcome) can reduce pressure and improve performance.
- You must adapt the plan's content focus (MBE, MEE, MPT slots) to match the specific subjects and components tested in your jurisdiction.

Part 1: Laying the Foundation (Pre-Week 1)

Chapter 1: Know Your Enemy - Understanding Your Bar Exam

Trying to prepare for the bar exam without first understanding exactly what it entails is remarkably silly, yet surprisingly common. It's like agreeing to a boxing match without knowing if your opponent is a lightweight or a heavyweight, how many rounds there are, or how the judges score the fight. You wouldn't do that, would you? (Well, maybe some people would, which perhaps explains a few things). To effectively use the 8-week schedule in this book, you absolutely must first get crystal clear on the specific beast you are about to confront. Don't assume you know. Don't rely on law school gossip. **Go to the source:** your state's bar examiners' website. Find their official information about the exam format, subjects, and scoring. Pretending the exam is something other than what it is because you *wish* it were different is a fast track to disappointment.

Decoding Your Jurisdictions Exam Format

Most bar exams in the United States have multiple parts, often spanning two days. While this book uses the Uniform Bar Exam (UBE) structure as a common reference point, you MUST verify the *exact* format for the state(s) where you plan to sit. Here's a breakdown of the typical components:

1. **The Multistate Bar Examination (MBE):** This is the multiple-choice behemoth.
    - **Format:** Typically 200 multiple-choice questions, administered over six hours (two 3-hour sessions of 100 questions each). That's about 1.8 minutes per question, folks – no time for leisurely contemplation or existential dread about your life choices.
    - **Subjects:** Covers seven core subjects: Civil Procedure, Constitutional Law, Contracts, Criminal Law and Procedure, Evidence, Real Property, and Torts. The National Conference of Bar Examiners (NCBE) website provides detailed outlines of what topics within these subjects are fair game.[5] Don't ignore these outlines! Believing you can just "wing it" based on your law school classes is irrational optimism at its finest.
    - **Question Style:** These aren't simple recall questions. They often involve a short factual scenario followed by a question requiring you to apply legal principles. They are designed to be tricky, with plausible-sounding wrong answers (distractors). Getting good at the MBE requires learning

the black-letter law *and* practicing the skill of reading carefully and eliminating wrong choices under time pressure.

2. **The Multistate Essay Examination (MEE) / State Essays:** This is where you show you can analyze a factual scenario and write a coherent legal argument.

    - **Format (UBE):** Typically consists of six essay questions administered in a three-hour session (30 minutes per essay). Some states use fewer MEE questions or substitute their own state-law essays. **Check your state's rules!**

    - **Subjects (UBE MEE):** Can test the seven MBE subjects *plus* Business Associations (Agency, Partnership, Corporations, LLCs), Conflict of Laws, Family Law, Trusts and Estates (Decedents' Estates; Trusts and Future Interests), and Uniform Commercial Code[6] Article 9 (Secured Transactions). That's a lot of ground to cover. Thinking "I'll just focus on the MBE subjects" is a terrible idea.

    - **State Essays:** If your state isn't purely UBE, it likely has its own essays testing specific state laws (e.g., state civil procedure, community property, oil and gas law – whatever delightful local specialties exist). You MUST identify and prepare for these.

    - **Expected Answer Style:** Bar examiners generally look for a structured answer format, like IRAC (Issue, Rule, Analysis, Conclusion) or variations like CRAC/CREAC. They want to see you spot the issues, state the relevant legal rules correctly, apply those rules to the specific facts, and reach a logical conclusion. Just dumping rules onto the page won't cut it. Writing essays is a *skill* that requires practice, practice, and—you guessed it—more practice.

3. **The Multistate Performance Test (MPT) / State Performance Test:** This section tests practical lawyering skills, not substantive law recall.

    - **Format (UBE):** Typically includes two MPT items administered in a three-hour session (90 minutes per item).[11] Again, **check your state**, as some use only one MPT or have their own state-specific performance tests.

- **Task:** You receive a "File" containing case documents (memos, depositions, client letters, etc.) and a "Library" containing relevant statutes, cases, or regulations (which may or may not all be pertinent!). Your task is to complete a specific assignment based on these materials, such as drafting a persuasive brief, an objective memorandum, a client letter, a contract provision, or a closing argument.
- **Skills Tested:** This isn't about knowing the law; it's about *using* the law provided to you. Can you sort through facts? Can you identify relevant legal principles from the Library? Can you follow instructions in the assigning memo? Can you organize your thoughts logically? Can you write clearly and persuasively (or objectively, depending on the task) under time pressure? Many students foolishly neglect the MPT, thinking it's "easy" because the law is provided. This is a dangerous misconception. Ninety minutes disappear incredibly fast. Mastering the MPT requires a specific strategy for reading, outlining, and writing efficiently.[12]

Scenario: James's Misstep

James was taking the bar in a UBE state. He heard from upperclassmen that "it's all about the MBE," so he spent 80% of his early prep time drilling multiple-choice questions. He vaguely knew there were essays and something called an MPT, but figured he'd "pick those up later." When he finally attempted an MPT three weeks before the exam, he was stunned. He couldn't even finish reading the File and Library in 90 minutes, let alone write a coherent answer. Panic set in. He'd ignored a huge chunk of the exam based on hearsay and wishful thinking, creating entirely unnecessary suffering for himself. Don't be James. Know your enemy—all parts of it.

Scoring Breakdown Where Points Come From

Understanding how the exam is scored is not just academic curiosity; it informs your study strategy. Again, **verify your specific jurisdiction's scoring**, but here's the typical UBE breakdown:

- **MBE:** Usually weighted at **50%** of the total score. Your raw score (number correct out of 175 scored questions – 25 are experimental) is scaled based on the difficulty of that particular test administration.[13]

- **MEE:** Usually weighted at **30%** of the total score (or 5% per essay if there are six). Graders score each essay, often on a scale (e.g., 1-6), and these scores are then scaled and combined.
- **MPT:** Usually weighted at **20%** of the total score (or 10% per item if there are two). Similar to essays, these are graded, scaled, and combined.

What does this weighting tell you?

1. **The MBE is undeniably important.** A strong MBE score provides a solid foundation. You cannot afford to neglect it.
2. **The written portion (MEE + MPT) is equally important.** Together, they make up the *other* 50% in a UBE jurisdiction! Many capable students fail because they focus too much on the MBE and neglect developing their writing and analytical skills for the essays and MPT. Telling yourself "I'm bad at writing, so I'll just ace the MBE" is irrational. You need competence across the board.
3. **You don't need perfection.** Bar passage scores vary by state, but they are *never* 100%. They are often somewhere in the range of needing roughly 65-70% competence overall (this is a simplification due to scaling, but captures the idea). This means you can get a significant number of questions wrong and still pass. Demanding that you *must* get every question right or write perfect essays is a form of perfectionism that generates anxiety and hinders performance. Aim for **competence across all sections**, not impossible brilliance in one.

Scenario: Sarah's Balancing Act

Sarah knew the scoring weights for her UBE state (50% MBE, 30% MEE, 20% MPT). Her diagnostic showed she was stronger on the MBE but weaker on essays and MPT timing. Instead of just doubling down on her MBE strength, she rationally decided to allocate slightly more time in her study schedule (using the framework in this book) to targeted essay practice and timed MPTs, while still diligently working on MBE questions. She didn't neglect her strength, but she deliberately shored up her weaknesses, recognizing they collectively accounted for half her score. This balanced approach served her far better than ignoring the writing components would have.

Identifying High Frequency Topics

While the bar examiners can theoretically test anything within the published subject outlines, reality shows that certain topics and sub-topics appear much more frequently than others. Negligence on the Torts essay? Highly likely. The Rule Against Perpetuities on a Real Property essay? Less likely (though not impossible, unfortunately for us all).

How do you figure out what's commonly tested?

- **NCBE Subject Matter Outlines:** Start here. The NCBE website provides detailed outlines for MBE and MEE subjects. Pay attention to the main headings and subheadings – these represent the universe of testable material.
- **Past Exam Questions/Summaries:** Many jurisdictions release past essay and MPT questions. Reviewing these (especially from the last 5-10 years) gives you a feel for the types of issues commonly tested and the depth of knowledge expected. Some commercial companies also compile analyses of topic frequency.
- **Commercial Bar Prep Materials:** Major bar prep providers often analyze topic frequency based on past exams and incorporate this into their materials, sometimes even providing frequency charts.[17] Use these as a guide, but not gospel.

Why does this matter?

Knowing high-frequency topics helps you prioritize your studying rationally. It does NOT mean you should only study those topics. That would be foolishly gambling. But it does mean you should ensure your understanding of core, frequently tested areas like negligence (Torts), formation/performance/breach (Contracts), hearsay (Evidence), subject matter/personal jurisdiction (Civil Procedure), corporate formation/director duties (Business Associations), etc., is absolutely solid. You should allocate more time and practice to these areas than to obscure, rarely tested doctrines.

Challenging the "Equal Study" Myth:

Some people operate under the irrational belief that they must give equal time and weight to every single topic listed in the outlines. This is inefficient and often impossible within an 8-week timeframe. It's far more rational to aim for deep mastery of the high-frequency areas and solid competence in the medium-frequency areas, while having a basic familiarity (recognize the issue, state a basic rule) with the low-frequency topics. You play the odds, intelligently. Don't "awfulize" if you don't feel like an expert on future interests—focus on making sure you can crush a negligence essay.

So, your first mission, before even touching Week 1, is to become an expert on the *structure* and *scope* of your specific bar exam. Get the facts. Know the format, understand the scoring, and get a sense of the most common battlegrounds. This factual grounding will dispel fear-based myths and allow you to approach your preparation logically.

Facing Facts The Exam Deconstructed

Alright, you've now got the basic intelligence report on the enemy. It might seem like a lot—multiple components, broad subjects, tricky scoring. It *is* a lot. But it's **knowable**. And knowing it prevents you from wasting time preparing for the wrong fight or ignoring critical parts of the assessment. Accepting the reality of the exam's structure and demands, without unnecessary dread or demands for it to be easier, is the first rational step. Now that you understand the battlefield, the next step is to gather the tools and supplies you'll need for the campaign ahead.

Key Takeaways for Chapter 1

- Do not start studying without confirming the exact format, subjects, and timing for *your* jurisdiction's bar exam directly from the official bar examiners' website.
- Understand the components: MBE (timed multiple-choice across 7 core subjects), MEE/State Essays (timed essays testing MBE subjects plus others, requiring structured analysis like IRAC), and MPT/Performance Test (timed practical skills test using provided File and Library).
- Know your exam's scoring weights (e.g., UBE is typically 50% MBE, 30% MEE, 20% MPT). Recognize that competence across *all* sections is needed; you generally can't pass by acing one part and failing others.
- You don't need perfection to pass. Aim for solid competence (often around 65-70% overall, pre-scaling) rather than demanding impossible brilliance.
- Identify high-frequency topics using official outlines, past questions, and potentially commercial prep analysis to prioritize your study time rationally.

Master the common areas while maintaining familiarity with less common ones.

- Avoid irrational beliefs like "I only need to study the MBE," "The MPT is easy," or "I must study every topic equally." Face the facts of the exam.

Chapter 2: Assembling Your Arsenal - Resources and Study Environment

Knowing the enemy is step one. Step two is gathering your weapons and fortifying your position. Going into the 8-week bar prep sprint without the right materials and a functional study space is like charging into battle armed with a wet noodle and wearing pajamas – you're making things needlessly difficult (and slightly ridiculous). People often get bogged down here, either by trying to acquire *every* possible resource out of anxiety ("What if I miss the *one* magic outline?!") or by neglecting to set up a decent workspace ("I can just study on the couch, right?"). Let's approach this sensibly. Your goal is to get **adequate, functional tools and a workable space**, not a perfect, gold-plated, unicorn-powered study system.

Choosing Your Core Materials

The bar prep market is flooded with options: massive commercial courses, standalone outlines, question banks, flashcards, workshops, tutors... it's enough to make your head spin and your wallet weep. The irrational belief that "more is always better" often leads students down a rabbit hole of conflicting advice and overwhelming stacks of paper. This is counterproductive. You need **one core set of substantive law outlines** and **one primary source of practice questions (MBE, Essay, MPT)**.

1. **Core Substantive Outlines:**
    - **Full Commercial Course:** Companies like Barbri, Kaplan, Themis, etc., offer all-in-one packages with outlines, lectures, and practice questions.[20]
        - *Pros:* Integrated system, often includes a schedule (though you'll be using *this* book's schedule!), covers all likely subjects.
        - *Cons:* Can be expensive, may provide *too much* detail leading to overwhelm, lecture pace might not suit everyone.
    - **Standalone Outlines:** You can buy outlines separately (e.g., commercial course outlines bought used, Emanuel Law Outlines, specific subject hornbooks – though hornbooks are often too detailed for primary bar prep).[21]
        - *Pros:* Potentially cheaper, allows mixing and matching.

        - *Cons:* Requires more effort to ensure complete subject coverage, might lack integration with practice questions.
    - **The Key:** Choose **one primary source** for your outlines. Don't try to learn Contracts from three different books simultaneously. It breeds confusion and wastes time. Pick a set that seems clear and comprehensive *enough* for you, and **stick with it**. You can *supplement* later for weak areas, but establish your main resource first.

2. **Practice Questions & Explanations:** This is non-negotiable. Active learning requires doing questions, lots of them.
    - **MBE Questions:** You need access to a large bank of MBE questions, ideally including **released questions from the NCBE** (the people who write the actual exam).[22] Explanations for *why* answers are right or wrong are absolutely essential.
        - *Sources:* Commercial courses include these. Online platforms like UWorld (formerly Themis UBE), AdaptiBar, or the NCBE's own BarNow platform offer large Q-banks, often with sophisticated performance tracking.[23] Standalone books of questions exist but lack the feedback features of online platforms.
        - **Recommendation:** An online platform with licensed NCBE questions and detailed explanations is highly recommended for its efficiency and feedback capabilities.
    - **Essay Questions:** You need access to past MEE questions (if in a UBE state) or state-specific essay questions. The NCBE releases MEE question banks. Your state bar website might release past state essays. Commercial courses provide these too. You also need **model answers or grading rubrics** to compare your work against. Merely writing essays without feedback is unproductive.
    - **MPT Questions:** Similar to essays, you need past MPTs (available from the NCBE or commercial providers) and the accompanying **model answers or point sheets** provided by the examiners.[24]

Scenario: Lisa's Resource Overload

Lisa, anxious about failing, bought access to two major bar prep courses and several standalone supplements. She spent her first week frantically trying to cross-reference outlines, watch lectures from both courses, and figure out which practice platform she liked better. She ended up feeling completely overwhelmed, behind schedule before she even started, and convinced she was doomed because she couldn't possibly absorb everything. Her irrational belief that she must use all available resources to succeed was sabotaging her. The rational approach? Pick one comprehensive course or a well-chosen set of primary materials (outline source + Q-bank) and commit. You can always add a small supplement later if a specific weak area emerges. Don't drown yourself in options.

Essential Study Tools

Beyond the core content materials, you need a few basic tools to facilitate your study process. Keep it simple and functional.

- **Reliable Timer:** Absolutely essential for practicing under timed conditions. Don't rely on your phone – too many distractions. Get a simple digital kitchen timer or a dedicated study timer. You need to internalize the feeling of 1.8 minutes per MBE question and 30/90 minutes for essays/MPTs.
- **Notebooks/Legal Pads or Digital Equivalent:** You'll need space for taking notes, outlining answers, brainstorming, and tracking progress. Physical paper works well for many; others prefer digital notes (like OneNote or Evernote). Choose what works for you, but have a system. Don't scribble notes randomly on scrap paper you'll lose.
- **Highlighters/Pens:** If using physical materials, a highlighting *system* can be useful (e.g., one color for rules, another for exceptions, another for policy). But avoid turning your outlines into abstract art – highlighting everything highlights nothing. Use pens for active note-taking and practice writing.
- **Computer/Laptop:** Necessary for accessing online question banks, viewing lectures (if applicable), and typing practice essays/MPTs (as most exams are now computer-based). Ensure it's reliable! Technical difficulties are an unnecessary source of stress.
- **Distraction-Blocking Software (Optional but Recommended):** If you struggle with the siren call of the internet (and who doesn't?), consider using apps like Freedom, Cold Turkey, or SelfControl to block distracting websites and

applications during scheduled study blocks. This is a practical tool to support your self-discipline.

Don't get bogged down in finding the "perfect" pen or the "prettiest" notebook. Get functional tools and move on. The goal is studying, not accessorizing.

Creating Your Optimal Study Space

Where you study significantly impacts your focus and efficiency. Trying to master complex legal rules amidst chaos is fighting an uphill battle. Your goal is a space that **minimizes distractions** and **signals to your brain that it's time to work**.

- **Location, Location, Location:**
  - **Ideal:** A dedicated room or corner in your home where you *only* study. This helps create a psychological association between the space and focus.
  - **Workable:** A library cubicle, a quiet corner of a coffee shop (with noise-canceling headphones perhaps), or even your kitchen table *if* you can establish clear rules about minimizing interruptions during study hours.
  - **Avoid:** Your bed (terrible for sleep hygiene and focus), the living room couch with the TV on, or anywhere you're constantly interrupted.
- **Minimize Distractions:**
  - **Visual:** Clear clutter from your desk. A messy space can contribute to a messy mind. Keep only essential study materials within view. Face a wall if possible, rather than a window overlooking interesting street life.
  - **Auditory:** If you can't control noise levels (e.g., roommates, family, traffic), use earplugs or noise-canceling headphones. Some find instrumental music helpful; others need silence. Experiment, but avoid music with lyrics, which tends to interfere with reading comprehension and writing.
  - **Digital:** This is often the biggest culprit. Keep your phone **out of sight and on silent** (or use blocking software, as mentioned). Close unnecessary tabs on your computer. Turn off notifications. Treat your

study time like you're in the actual exam hall – no external communication allowed.

- **Comfort and Ergonomics (Within Reason):** A reasonably comfortable chair and adequate lighting are important to avoid physical strain over long hours. But don't use the quest for the "perfect ergonomic setup" as another form of procrastination. Functional is good enough.

Challenging the "Perfect Space" Myth:

Some people convince themselves they cannot possibly study effectively unless their environment is absolutely perfect – silent, aesthetically pleasing, with precisely brewed artisanal coffee. This is usually just an excuse born from anxiety or a reluctance to start. Your study space needs to be functional, not flawless. Accept that minor imperfections or distractions might occur, and practice refocusing your attention rather than demanding an impossible standard. Can you establish a space that is mostly quiet and relatively free from interruption for several hours at a time? Good. Start there.

Scenario: David's Distraction Battle

David tried studying at his shared apartment's kitchen table. His roommate constantly wandered in for snacks, the phone rang, delivery drivers knocked... He got frustrated, telling himself, "It's impossible to study here! I need total silence!" Instead of giving up or demanding the impossible, he took rational steps. He talked to his roommate about respecting specific "quiet hours." He put his phone in another room. He found some instrumental focus music for his headphones. Was it perfect? No. Was it functional enough to allow concentrated work? Yes. He adapted to reality instead of demanding reality conform to his preferences.

Setting up your arsenal isn't about spending a fortune or achieving perfection. It's about making **sensible choices** to acquire adequate materials and create a workable environment that supports, rather than hinders, the intense study effort required over the next eight weeks.

Gearing Up Sensibly

Okay, you've identified the enemy (Chapter 1) and now you've gathered your basic supplies and secured your base camp. You have your core legal texts, a way to practice actively, the necessary tools, and a space designed for focus. Resisting the urge to over-gather resources or demand a perfect environment is key. Good enough is truly good enough here. Now, with the battlefield surveyed and your equipment ready, it's time to figure out your specific starting position – your strengths, your weaknesses, and where you need to aim your efforts first. Let's move on to diagnostic assessment and goal setting.

Key Takeaways for Chapter 2

- Avoid resource overload. Choose **one primary set** of substantive law outlines and **one primary source** for practice questions (MBE, Essays, MPTs). Stick with them initially.
- Prioritize practice materials that include **licensed NCBE questions** (especially for MBE) and **detailed explanations** or model answers/grading guides.
- Essential tools are simple: a reliable **timer**, notebooks (physical or digital), basic writing implements, and a reliable computer. Distraction-blocking software is highly recommended.
- Create a dedicated study space that **minimizes distractions** (visual, auditory, digital).[26] Focus on functional and consistent, not perfect.
- Keep your phone out of sight and silent during study blocks. Treat study time like exam time regarding external communication.
- Challenge irrational beliefs like "More resources must be better" or "I need a perfect study environment." Make sensible choices, commit to them, and focus on functionality over flawless ideals.

Chapter 3: The Starting Line - Diagnostic Assessment and Goal Setting

Alright, you know what the bar exam looks like (Chapter 1) and you've gathered your study materials and set up your workspace (Chapter 2). Excellent. Now, before you plunge headfirst into Week 1 of the schedule, there's a critical—and often resisted—step: figuring out where you actually stand right now. Launching into a demanding study plan without knowing your current strengths and weaknesses is like setting off on a cross-country road trip without checking your fuel gauge or knowing which direction to head first. It's inefficient and potentially disastrous. Many people avoid this step because they irrationally fear seeing evidence of their weaknesses ("I *can't* bear to see how badly I'll do! It will prove I'm stupid!"). This is nonsense. A diagnostic test isn't a judgment; it's **data**. And data is your friend. It tells you where to focus your precious time and energy.

Taking a Diagnostic Test

The purpose of a diagnostic test is simple: to get a baseline measurement of your current abilities across the different sections of the bar exam **before** you start intensive studying. This isn't about getting a "good score"; it's about identifying areas needing the most work.

What should a good diagnostic include?

- **MBE Section:** At least 50-100 MBE questions, done under timed conditions (1.8 minutes per question). Ideally, use questions you haven't seen before, preferably released NCBE questions if possible. The goal is to simulate the time pressure and question style.
- **Essay Section:** Write out full answers to 1-2 MEE or state-specific essay questions, under timed conditions (typically 30 minutes per essay). Choose prompts representative of common subjects.
- **MPT Section:** Complete one MPT under timed conditions (90 minutes).Again, use a real MPT prompt you haven't encountered previously.

Where can you find diagnostic materials?

- **Commercial Bar Prep Courses:** Most full courses include a diagnostic test at the very beginning. Use it!

- **NCBE:** The National Conference of Bar Examiners sells study aids, including practice exams and individual questions (BarNow platform). You could assemble a diagnostic from these materials.
- **Standalone Resources:** Some bar prep supplements or tutors might offer diagnostic assessments.

The Process:

1. **Schedule It:** Set aside a specific block of time (likely 4-6 hours) to take the diagnostic under exam-like conditions. No distractions, strict timing.
2. **Simulate Conditions:** Do it seriously. Don't look up answers. Stick to the time limits rigidly. If you're taking the exam on computer, do the diagnostic practice on computer.
3. **Score It (Honestly):** Score your MBE section objectively. For the essays and MPT, use the model answers and grading rubrics/point sheets provided. Be brutally honest with yourself when comparing your work to the models. Did you spot the key issues? State the rules correctly? Apply the facts? Structure it logically? Give yourself an estimated score or rating (e.g., clearly failing, borderline, passing).

Scenario: Carlos Confronts Reality

Carlos breezed through Contracts in law school, got an A, and felt confident. He almost skipped doing Contracts questions on his diagnostic MBE, thinking it was a waste of time. He forced himself to do them anyway. The result? He scored only 45% correct. Stunned, he reviewed the explanations. He realized that while he knew the general concepts, he was shaky on specific nuances frequently tested on the MBE and kept falling for clever distractors. The diagnostic shattered his illusion of competence (a good thing!) and showed him that Contracts needed more attention than he initially assumed, not less. Ignoring this data would have been foolish.

Honest Self Assessment Identifying Strengths and Weaknesses

The diagnostic test gives you raw data. Now you need to analyze it honestly to identify patterns. Resisting this analysis because it might hurt your ego ("I *should* be good at everything!") is self-defeating. Acceptance of your current reality—warts and all—is the starting point for improvement.

How to Analyze:

1. **MBE Breakdown:** Don't just look at the overall MBE score. Break it down **by subject**. Most platforms do this automatically. Which subjects were your lowest scoring? Which were highest? Are there specific *types* of questions (e.g., those requiring close reading of statutes) you consistently miss across subjects?
2. **Essay Analysis:** Look at your practice essays critically using the model answers/rubrics.
   - **Issue Spotting:** Did you identify the main legal issues tested? Did you miss any? Did you discuss non-issues?
   - **Rule Statements:** Did you state the relevant black-letter law accurately and completely? Was it the *correct* rule for the issue?
   - **Analysis (Application):** Did you effectively apply the rules to the specific facts provided? Did you use the key facts? Was your reasoning logical? This is often the weakest area for students.
   - **Organization/Clarity:** Was your answer well-structured (e.g., IRAC)? Was it easy to read and understand? Did you manage your time effectively?
3. **MPT Analysis:** Review your MPT performance against the model answer/point sheet.
   - **Task Completion:** Did you do what the assigning memo asked (e.g., write a persuasive brief, an objective memo)? Did you follow formatting instructions?
   - **Using the File/Library:** Did you effectively extract the relevant facts from the File? Did you identify and apply the correct legal principles from the Library? Did you synthesize rules from multiple sources if needed?
   - **Analysis/Argument:** Was your reasoning sound? If persuasive, was the argument well-supported by the facts and law? If objective, was the analysis balanced?

- **Organization/Clarity/Timing:** Was the document well-organized? Clearly written? Did you finish (or get close) within the 90 minutes?

Categorize Your Areas:

Based on this analysis, create a simple list categorizing subjects and skills (MBE-by subject, Essay Writing, MPT Skills) into three buckets:

- **Weak:** Areas where you performed poorly on the diagnostic and feel significant lack of understanding or skill. These need the *most* attention.
- **Okay:** Areas where you performed adequately but not great. You have a basic grasp but need refinement and more practice.
- **Strong:** Areas where you performed well and feel relatively confident. These still need review and practice to maintain proficiency, but less intensive focus initially.

Embrace the Weakness:

Seeing areas marked "Weak" can be discouraging. You might tell yourself, "This proves I'll never pass!" Rubbish. It simply shows you where to direct your efforts most efficiently. Finding weaknesses now is a gift—it allows you to fix them over the next eight weeks. Finding them out on exam day is considerably less helpful. Accept the data without judgment and use it strategically.

Setting SMART Goals for the Next 8 Weeks

Okay, you have your baseline data and a list of strengths and weaknesses. Now, let's set some clear, actionable goals for your 8-week study period. Vague goals like "study hard" or "learn everything" are useless. They aren't measurable and provide no direction. We need **SMART** goals:

- **S**pecific: Clearly define what you want to accomplish. Not "get better at MBE," but "Increase overall MBE score." Even better: "Increase MBE Contracts score."
- **M**easurable: Define how you will track progress. Not "learn Torts," but "Consistently score 65%+ on Torts MBE practice sets" or "Write 3 passing-level Torts essays per week."
- **A**chievable (or Attainable): Be realistic given your starting point and the 8-week timeframe. Don't set a goal to score 95% on the MBE if your diagnostic

was 40%. Aim for significant, *possible* improvement. Setting impossible goals guarantees frustration ("I *must* achieve this impossible thing, and since I can't, I'm a failure!").[30] Aiming for "Improve MBE score from 50% to 65-70%" is challenging but likely achievable with consistent effort.

- **R**elevant: Ensure your goals directly relate to passing *your* specific bar exam. Goals should focus on improving performance on the tested subjects and skills.
- **T**ime-bound: Set deadlines. In this case, the overall deadline is the 8-week mark (exam day!), but you can set intermediate goals (e.g., "Reach 60% average on MBE by end of Week 4").

Examples of SMART Goals for Bar Prep:

- **Outcome Goal (MBE):** Increase overall MBE scaled score simulation from [Diagnostic Score]% to 68% by the end of Week 8, as measured by full-length timed practice exams.
- **Outcome Goal (Essays):** Be able to consistently write essays under timed conditions that would receive a passing score (e.g., a 4 out of 6 on the UBE scale) in my weakest subjects (identified as X, Y, Z) by Week 7, as assessed by self-grading against model answers and potentially tutor feedback.
- **Process Goal (Consistency):** Complete at least 90% of the scheduled practice questions (MBE, Essay, MPT) outlined in this book each week for the entire 8 weeks. (Process goals focus on your *effort* and *actions*, which are more within your control than specific scores).
- **Process Goal (Review):** Dedicate a minimum of 45 minutes each study day to actively reviewing explanations for incorrect MBE questions and comparing practice essays/MPTs to model answers.

Connecting Goals to Diagnostics:

Your SMART goals should directly address the weaknesses identified in your self-assessment. If Civil Procedure MBE was a disaster, a specific, measurable goal related to improving that score is essential. If MPT timing was your downfall, a goal focused on completing MPTs within the 90-minute limit is key.

Don't set too many goals – focus on the most critical areas for improvement. Write them down. Look at them regularly. They provide direction and motivation, turning the vague desire to "pass the bar" into concrete steps you can take each day.

Knowing Your Starting Point

Taking stock honestly—through diagnostics and clear-eyed assessment—isn't about judgment or prediction. It's about strategy. It's about gathering the intelligence needed to deploy your resources (time, energy, focus) effectively over the demanding weeks ahead. Setting SMART goals based on this intelligence transforms wishful thinking into a concrete plan of attack. Refusing to look at your weaknesses doesn't make them disappear; it just ensures you won't address them properly. Now that you know where you stand and where you need to go, the final piece of preparation involves shoring up your external environment and internal resilience for the intense journey. Let's talk logistics and well-being.

Key Takeaways for Chapter 3

- Taking a diagnostic test (timed MBE section, timed essays, timed MPT) before starting Week 1 is essential for identifying your baseline strengths and weaknesses.
- Approach the diagnostic as data gathering, not judgment. Use released NCBE materials or reliable commercial sources if possible.
- Analyze your diagnostic results *honestly*, breaking down MBE scores by subject and critically evaluating essay/MPT performance against model answers regarding issue spotting, rule statements, analysis, organization, and timing.
- Categorize subjects and skills into Weak, Okay, and Strong to guide your study focus. Don't fear weaknesses; see them as opportunities for targeted improvement.
- Set SMART goals (Specific, Measurable, Achievable, Relevant, Time-bound) based on your diagnostic assessment. Focus on both outcome goals (scores) and process goals (study habits).

- Ensure goals are realistic to avoid setting yourself up for frustration based on perfectionistic demands ("I *must* achieve X score!"). Aim for significant, possible improvement.
- Use your assessment and goals strategically to tailor how you approach the study schedule in the coming weeks.

Chapter 4: Preparing for the Sprint - Logistics and Well-being

You've analyzed the exam, gathered your resources, established your starting point, and set your goals. The internal groundwork is laid. Now, we need to address the external realities and your own internal state. An 8-week bar prep schedule is, let's be blunt, a grueling sprint. Trying to run it effectively while your life logistics are chaotic and your mental/physical well-being is crumbling is like trying to win a marathon with your shoelaces tied together while suffering from the flu. It's not smart, and it dramatically increases your chances of crashing and burning. This chapter is about proactively managing your environment and yourself to sustain the necessary effort. Ignoring this is often rooted in irrational beliefs like "I *should* be able to handle everything without special arrangements" or "Focusing on well-being is weak; I *must* just push through." This thinking is foolish and counterproductive.

Clearing Your Calendar Minimizing External Commitments

For the next eight weeks, bar study **must** be your primary, almost singular, focus. This requires a level of temporary selfishness that might feel uncomfortable, but it's necessary. You cannot realistically maintain a full social life, extensive hobbies, demanding side projects, or numerous external obligations *and* successfully execute this intensive study plan. Trying to do it all is a recipe for exhaustion, resentment, and likely failure on the bar exam front.

Action Steps:

1. **Identify All Commitments:** Go through your calendar for the next eight weeks with a red pen. List everything: work obligations (if applicable), family events, social gatherings, appointments, volunteer activities, regular meetings, etc.
2. **Categorize Ruthlessly:** Divide the list into three categories:
    - **Absolutely Non-Negotiable:** Things you truly cannot get out of (e.g., critical work deadlines if studying while working, a close family member's wedding – maybe). Be extremely strict here.
    - **Negotiable/Postponable:** Things that can potentially be rescheduled, delegated, or skipped (e.g., routine appointments, social dinners, committee meetings, most volunteer work).

- **Eliminate:** Things you will simply cancel or decline for the next eight weeks (e.g., casual meetups, book club, new projects, most travel).

3. **Act Immediately:** Start clearing the decks *now*. Reschedule appointments. Politely decline invitations. Delegate tasks if possible. Inform groups or organizations you won't be available. The goal is to free up as much time and mental energy as possible. Every "yes" to an external commitment during this period is effectively a "no" to study time or essential rest.

Why is this so important?

- **Focus:** Constant context-switching between studying and other obligations fragments your attention and reduces learning efficiency.[32]
- **Energy:** Every commitment drains mental and emotional energy. You need to conserve that energy for studying.
- **Decision Fatigue:** Having fewer decisions to make about non-study activities frees up cognitive resources for tackling complex legal rules.

Scenario: Priya's Prioritization Problem

Priya felt guilty saying no. She tried to keep up her weekly volunteering commitment, her pottery class, and regular dinners with friends during her 8-week study period. She thought she should be able to balance it all. What happened? She was constantly tired, rushed her studying, felt resentful of her commitments but also guilty about wanting to drop them, and her practice scores stagnated. She was spreading herself too thin because she hadn't accepted the necessity of temporary, focused sacrifice. Don't make Priya's mistake. Be polite, but be firm. These eight weeks are different.

Communicating with Your Support System

You likely have people in your life—family, partners, close friends, possibly employers or colleagues—who form your support system. They can be a tremendous asset during bar prep, or (often unintentionally) a significant source of stress and distraction if expectations aren't managed. Clear, honest communication *before* you start the 8-week sprint is essential. Don't assume they magically understand what you need or how demanding this process is.

What to Communicate:

1. **The Intensity and Duration:** Explain that you're undertaking a very demanding, full-time (or more!) study schedule for the next eight weeks. Emphasize it's temporary but requires significant focus.
2. **Your Limited Availability:** Be explicit about what this means in practice. "I won't be able to socialize much." "I'll need uninterrupted blocks of time for studying." "My contribution to household chores might need to decrease temporarily (and discuss how to manage this)." "Please don't take it personally if I seem stressed or preoccupied."
3. **What Support Looks Like (Be Specific):** Tell them how they *can* help. This might be:
   - Respecting your study schedule and designated quiet times/space.
   - Helping with practical things like meals or errands occasionally.[33]
   - Offering encouragement and understanding (without constantly asking "How's studying going?" which can add pressure).
   - Simply *not* adding extra demands or guilt trips during this period.
4. **Managing Expectations (Yours and Theirs):** Acknowledge that this will be tough on them too. Thank them in advance for their patience. Importantly, challenge *your own* irrational beliefs like "They *must* understand perfectly" or "They *should* anticipate my needs without me asking." People aren't mind-readers. Clear communication is your responsibility. Also, don't demand perfect support; aim for good-enough understanding and cooperation.

Scenario: Ben Gets Specific

Ben's partner initially felt neglected when Ben started his intense study schedule. Ben had just said he'd be "busy." This vague statement led to misunderstandings. After a tense week, Ben sat down and explained specifically: "From 8 AM to 6 PM on weekdays, I need to be completely focused in the study room, please try not to interrupt me unless it's urgent. It would be a huge help if you could handle dinner on Tuesdays and Thursdays. I know this is a big ask, and I really appreciate your support for these next seven weeks." This specific, honest conversation cleared the air and allowed his partner to offer targeted support, reducing friction for both of them.

Establishing a Routine Sleep Nutrition Exercise

Consistency and predictability are your allies during this stressful period. Establishing a solid daily routine helps automate basic decisions, conserves mental energy, and supports your physical and cognitive functioning. Winging it day-to-day increases stress and reduces efficiency.

- **Sleep:** This is non-negotiable. Sacrificing sleep to cram more study hours is incredibly counterproductive. Sleep deprivation tanks your cognitive function, memory consolidation, mood regulation, and immune system.
    - **Goal:** Aim for 7-9 hours of **consistent** sleep per night.
    - **Routine:** Go to bed and wake up around the same time every day, even on weekends. Create a relaxing pre-sleep ritual (e.g., reading something non-law related, dimming lights, avoiding screens).[36] Protect your sleep schedule as fiercely as you protect your study time. Believing "I *must* study more, even if it means less sleep" is a biologically foolish idea.
- **Nutrition:** Your brain needs fuel to function optimally. Relying on caffeine, sugar, and junk food will lead to energy crashes and impair concentration.
    - **Goal:** Eat regular, reasonably balanced meals and snacks.
    - **Routine:** Plan simple meals ahead of time to avoid decision fatigue or skipping meals. Keep healthy snacks on hand (nuts, fruit, yogurt). Stay hydrated – drink plenty of water. Don't use food as a primary coping mechanism for stress. Treat your body like the machine it needs to be to get through this.
- **Exercise:** Physical activity is one of the most effective ways to manage stress, boost energy levels, and improve cognitive function.[38] It's not a luxury; it's a necessity for sustainable performance.
    - **Goal:** Incorporate some form of movement into most days. This doesn't mean training for a marathon.
    - **Routine:** Schedule short bursts of activity – a brisk 20-30 minute walk outside, a quick home workout, stretching breaks. Even brief movement helps clear your head and reset your focus. Find something you tolerate or even slightly enjoy and build it into your daily schedule *as if it were a study block*. Telling yourself "I don't have time to

exercise" is ignoring a powerful tool for enhancing the *quality* of your study time.

Mental Health Strategy Managing Stress and Preventing Burnout

Let's be realistic: bar prep is stressful. You *will* feel anxious, overwhelmed, frustrated, and doubtful at times. Pretending you won't, or demanding that you *must* feel calm and confident always, is irrational and sets you up for feeling worse when those normal human emotions inevitably arise. The goal isn't to eliminate stress; it's to **manage it effectively** so it doesn't derail you. This requires proactive strategies, not just reacting when you're already melting down.

Core Components of a Mental Health Strategy:

1. **Acknowledge and Accept Feelings:** Recognize that anxiety, frustration, etc., are *normal* responses to a high-stakes, demanding situation. Don't judge yourself for feeling them ("I *shouldn't* feel anxious!"). Acceptance ("Okay, I'm feeling anxious right now") reduces the secondary suffering caused by fighting your own emotions.[39]

2. **Challenge Irrational Thoughts:** This is key. Much of your emotional distress comes not directly from the bar exam itself, but from the *nonsense you tell yourself about it*. Pay attention to your self-talk. When you feel overly anxious or hopeless, ask: "What am I telling myself right now?" Identify the irrational beliefs (often involving "must," "should," "awful," "terrible," "can't stand it," "prove I'm worthless") and actively dispute them.

    - *Example Belief:* "If I fail this practice set, it means I'm going to fail the bar exam, and that would be *awful* and *prove* I'm incompetent!"

    - *Rational Challenge:* "Failing a practice set is disappointing, but it doesn't *prove* I'll fail the bar. It just shows I need more work in this area. It's information. Failing the bar would be highly inconvenient and frustrating, but not *awful* in the grand scheme of life, and it certainly wouldn't define my entire worth as a person. I can stand the discomfort of studying and the possibility of failure, even though I strongly prefer to pass."

3. **Schedule Regular Breaks:** Build **real breaks** into your daily schedule.[40] Not just switching from Torts to Contracts, but stepping away completely. Short breaks

every hour (5-10 mins) and a longer break mid-day (30-60 mins) are essential. Use this time to move, get fresh air, listen to music, meditate, or do something totally unrelated to law. Protect these breaks!

4. **Maintain Perspective:** Remind yourself frequently that the bar exam, while significant, is only one event in your life. It does not define your intelligence, your worth, or your entire future happiness (despite what your anxious brain might scream). Connect with things outside of bar prep, even briefly, to maintain perspective.

5. **Utilize Coping Mechanisms:** Have a short list of healthy coping tools ready for when stress spikes:

    - Deep breathing exercises (simple, fast, effective).
    - Short mindfulness meditation (apps like Calm or Headspace can help).
    - Physical activity (a quick walk, jumping jacks).
    - Talking briefly to a *supportive* friend or family member (not someone who increases your anxiety).
    - Listening to uplifting music.

6. **Know When to Seek Help:** If stress becomes overwhelming, persistently interferes with your functioning, or you experience significant symptoms of depression or anxiety, **seek professional help** from a therapist or counselor. Doing so is a sign of strength and rational self-care, not weakness.

Proactively managing logistics and well-being isn't coddling yourself; it's **strategic preparation**. It's about creating the conditions—both external and internal—that allow you to perform at your best during this demanding 8-week period.

Setting the Stage for Sanity and Success

You've done the prep work. You understand the exam, you have your tools, you know your starting point and goals, and you've hopefully taken concrete steps to clear your schedule, communicate with your support system, establish routines, and prepare a mental health strategy. This foundation is absolutely necessary for navigating the intense schedule ahead. It’s about controlling what you *can* control – your preparation, your environment, your routines, and crucially, your *thinking* about the unavoidable challenges. With this groundwork laid, you are now truly ready to begin the 8-week sprint itself. Let the structured work commence.

Key Takeaways for Chapter 4

- Ruthlessly clear your calendar of non-essential commitments for the 8-week study period to conserve focus and energy. Prioritize bar study above almost everything else temporarily.
- Communicate clearly and proactively with your support system (family, friends, employers) about the intensity of the schedule, your limited availability, and specific ways they can offer support (and what isn't helpful). Manage expectations – yours and theirs.
- Establish and maintain a consistent daily routine, prioritizing 7-9 hours of sleep, regular balanced nutrition, and short bursts of physical activity. Routine reduces decision fatigue and supports cognitive function.
- Develop a proactive mental health strategy: acknowledge and accept stress as normal, actively challenge irrational thoughts (especially "musts" and "awfulizing"), schedule regular *real* breaks, maintain perspective, and utilize healthy coping mechanisms.
- Don't hesitate to seek professional help if stress becomes unmanageable. This is a rational act of self-care.
- Preparing logistics and well-being isn't optional; it's a strategic necessity for sustaining effort and maximizing performance during the demanding 8-week schedule.

Part 2: The 8-Week Daily Breakdown

Here begins Part 2, the core of this book – the day-by-day, week-by-week plan. You've done the essential groundwork: understanding the exam, gathering your tools, assessing your starting point, setting goals, and preparing your life and mind for the intensity to come. Now, it's time to execute.

These next eight chapters represent the eight weeks of the study schedule. Each chapter follows a consistent structure: a weekly overview (goals, subjects, tasks, mindset tip), a detailed daily schedule (morning, afternoon, evening blocks), and a note on the weekend structure.

A crucial point before we start Week 1: **Stick to the schedule as consistently as humanly possible.** Life happens, yes, and we discussed rational adaptability back in the Introduction. But don't use "adaptability" as an excuse for procrastination or avoiding difficult tasks. The structure is designed to ensure comprehensive coverage and balanced practice. Deviating significantly, especially early on, undermines the entire process. You might feel overwhelmed initially. You might think, "This is too fast!" or "I don't understand this topic perfectly yet!" Tough. Keep moving. Follow the plan. Do the work. Perfection is not the goal; consistent, focused effort is. Let's begin.

Chapter 5: Week 1 - Building the Base

Welcome to Week 1. This is where the rubber meets the road. The primary goals this week are to **establish a consistent study rhythm**, begin covering two foundational MBE subjects (Torts and Contracts), and get introduced to the basic formats and skills required for essays and the MPT. Don't expect mastery yet—that's irrational. Expect to feel a bit lost, maybe overwhelmed, and definitely tired by the end of the week. That's normal. Your job is to show up each day, follow the schedule, do the assigned tasks, and start building the mental muscles needed for this marathon sprint. Resistance and discomfort are part of the process; accept them and keep working.

Weekly Overview

- **Goals for the Week:**
    - Establish and follow the daily study routine consistently.
    - Cover core concepts of Intentional Torts, Negligence (Duty, Breach, Causation, Damages), and Contract Formation (Offer, Acceptance, Consideration).
    - Complete approximately 175-200 targeted MBE questions on Torts and Contracts.
    - Understand the basic IRAC structure for essay writing and practice applying it to one Torts and one Contracts essay (untimed initially).
    - Familiarize yourself with the MPT format by analyzing one sample task (objective memo).
    - Develop the habit of reviewing incorrect answers daily.
- **Subjects Covered:**
    - MBE/Essays: Torts (Intentional Torts, Negligence), Contracts (Formation).
    - Skills: Basic Essay Structuring (IRAC), MPT Format Introduction (Objective Memo).
- **Key Tasks:**
    - Daily substantive review per schedule (approx. 1.5-2 hours/day).

    - Daily targeted MBE practice (approx. 25-30 questions/day).
    - Complete 1 untimed Torts essay, 1 untimed Contracts essay (focus on structure).
    - Analyze 1 MPT task (objective memo format and requirements).
    - Daily review of incorrect answers/model answers (approx. 1-1.5 hours/day).
- **Mindset Focus for the Week: Combatting "Perfection Paralysis"**
    - You might tell yourself, "I *must* understand Torts perfectly before I move on!" or "I *must* get all these MBE questions right!" This is perfectionistic nonsense that leads to getting stuck or feeling hopeless.
    - **Challenge:** Your goal this week is **familiarity and initial practice**, not flawless mastery. It's okay—no, it's *expected*—that you won't grasp everything instantly. It's okay to get questions wrong; that's how you learn!
    - **Rational Alternative:** "I *prefer* to understand everything easily, but I accept that learning takes time and repetition. My task is to follow the schedule, engage with the material, do the practice, and review my errors. Understanding will build gradually. Getting questions wrong provides valuable feedback." **Just start, and keep going.**

Daily Schedule Day 1 - Day 7

(Note: Adjust start/end times based on your personal rhythm, but maintain the approximate block durations and sequence.)

Day 1: Monday

- **Morning Block (e.g., 8:30 AM - 12:30 PM):**
    - **Substantive Review (1.5 hrs):** Torts - Introduction & Intentional Torts (Battery, Assault, False Imprisonment, IIED, Trespass to Land/Chattels, Conversion). Focus on elements of each.

- **MBE Practice (1.5 hrs):** 25-30 MBE questions specifically on Intentional Torts. Time yourself loosely (aim for ~2 min/question), but focus now is on understanding *how* these are tested.
- **Brief Review (30 mins):** Quick scan of incorrect answers from MBE set. Identify patterns.

- **Afternoon Block (e.g., 1:30 PM - 5:00 PM):**
  - **Skills Intro (1 hr):** Essay Writing - Read about the IRAC (or CRAC/CREAC) method. Find a sample Torts essay question on Intentional Torts. Don't write it yet, just read the question and the model answer, specifically looking for how it uses IRAC structure.
  - **Substantive Review (1.5 hrs):** Torts - Defenses to Intentional Torts (Consent, Self-Defense, Defense of Others/Property).
  - **MBE Practice (1 hr):** 15-20 MBE questions on Defenses to Intentional Torts.
- **Evening Block (e.g., 6:00 PM - 7:30 PM):**
  - **Review (1.5 hrs):** Thoroughly review explanations for *all* incorrect MBE questions from the day. Make brief notes on rules you missed or misunderstood. Consolidate Torts notes.

Day 2: Tuesday

- **Morning Block (e.g., 8:30 AM - 12:30 PM):**
  - **Substantive Review (1.5 hrs):** Torts - Negligence: Duty (General duty, affirmative duties, landowners, professionals).
  - **MBE Practice (1.5 hrs):** 25-30 MBE questions specifically on Negligence (Duty).
  - **Brief Review (30 mins):** Quick scan of incorrect MBE answers.
- **Afternoon Block (e.g., 1:30 PM - 5:00 PM):**
  - **Substantive Review (1.5 hrs):** Torts - Negligence: Breach (Reasonable person standard, negligence per se, res ipsa loquitur).

- **MBE Practice (1 hr):** 15-20 MBE questions on Negligence (Breach).
- **Essay Practice (1 hr):** Take that Torts essay question from yesterday (or a new one on Duty/Breach). **Untimed**, write out a full answer focusing *only* on applying the IRAC structure clearly for each issue you spot. Don't worry about perfection, focus on the format: Issue stated? Rule stated? Application to facts? Conclusion?

- **Evening Block (e.g., 6:00 PM - 7:30 PM):**
  - **Review (1.5 hrs):** Review incorrect MBEs from the day. Compare your practice essay to the model answer – focus on structure and rule statements. Where did you deviate? What did you miss? Consolidate Negligence notes.

Day 3: Wednesday

- **Morning Block (e.g., 8:30 AM - 12:30 PM):**
  - **Substantive Review (1.5 hrs):** Torts - Negligence: Causation (Actual/"But-For" Cause, Proximate/"Legal" Cause, intervening/superseding causes). This is tricky stuff – go slow.
  - **MBE Practice (1.5 hrs):** 25-30 MBE questions specifically on Negligence (Causation). Expect confusion here, it's normal.
  - **Brief Review (30 mins):** Quick scan of incorrect MBEs.
- **Afternoon Block (e.g., 1:30 PM - 5:00 PM):**
  - **Substantive Review (1.5 hrs):** Torts - Negligence: Damages (Compensatory, punitive, mitigation). Defenses to Negligence (Contributory Negligence, Comparative Fault, Assumption of Risk).
  - **MBE Practice (1 hr):** 15-20 MBE questions on Negligence (Damages & Defenses).
  - **Skills Intro (1 hr):** MPT Introduction - Find a sample MPT question that requires an Objective Memorandum. Read the Task Memo carefully. Read through the File and Library, just to get a feel for the documents. Don't write yet. What is the assigning attorney asking for? What's the requested format?

- **Evening Block (e.g., 6:00 PM - 7:30 PM):**
  - **Review (1.5 hrs):** Thorough review of incorrect MBEs (especially Causation!). Look at the MPT model answer – how did it structure the objective memo? What headings did it use? Consolidate Torts notes.

Day 4: Thursday

- **Morning Block (e.g., 8:30 AM - 12:30 PM):**
  - **Substantive Review (1.5 hrs):** Contracts - Introduction & Applicable Law (UCC vs. Common Law), Contract Formation Overview, Offer.
  - **MBE Practice (1.5 hrs):** 25-30 MBE questions specifically on Contracts (Applicable Law, Offer).
  - **Brief Review (30 mins):** Quick scan of incorrect MBEs.
- **Afternoon Block (e.g., 1:30 PM - 5:00 PM):**
  - **Substantive Review (1.5 hrs):** Contracts - Acceptance (Mirror image rule, UCC 2-207 Battle of the Forms, Mailbox Rule).
  - **MBE Practice (1 hr):** 15-20 MBE questions on Contracts (Acceptance).
  - **Essay Practice (1 hr):** Find a Contracts essay question on Formation (Offer/Acceptance). **Untimed**, write a full IRAC answer. Focus on identifying the issues (Is there an offer? Was it terminated? Was there valid acceptance?) and applying the rules.
- **Evening Block (e.g., 6:00 PM - 7:30 PM):**
  - **Review (1.5 hrs):** Review incorrect MBEs. Compare your Contracts essay to the model answer. Check your IRAC structure and rule statements carefully. Start consolidating Contracts notes.

Day 5: Friday

- **Morning Block (e.g., 8:30 AM - 12:30 PM):**
  - **Substantive Review (1.5 hrs):** Contracts - Consideration (Bargained-for exchange, legal detriment/benefit, pre-existing duty rule, modifications).

  - **MBE Practice (1.5 hrs):** 25-30 MBE questions specifically on Contracts (Consideration).
  - **Brief Review (30 mins):** Quick scan of incorrect MBEs.
- **Afternoon Block (e.g., 1:30 PM - 5:00 PM):**
  - **Substantive Review (1.5 hrs):** Contracts - Consideration Substitutes (Promissory Estoppel, quasi-contract). Defenses to Formation (Mistake, Misunderstanding, Misrepresentation/Fraud, Duress, Undue Influence – intro only).
  - **MBE Practice (1 hr):** 15-20 MBE questions on Contracts (Consideration Substitutes, basic Defenses).
  - **MPT Practice (1 hr):** Look back at the MPT Objective Memo task from Wednesday. This time, try to **outline** an answer based on the File and Library. Don't write the full memo yet. Just structure the headings and note the key facts/rules you would include under each. Compare your outline to the structure of the model answer.
- **Evening Block (e.g., 6:00 PM - 7:30 PM):**
  - **Review (1.5 hrs):** Thorough review of incorrect MBEs. Review your MPT outline against the model. Did you organize it logically based on the task memo? Consolidate Contracts notes.

Day 6: Saturday

- **Morning Block (e.g., 9:00 AM - 12:30 PM):**
  - **Mixed MBE Practice (2 hrs):** 50 MBE questions, timed (aim for 90 minutes). Mix of Torts and Contracts questions from the entire week. Simulate test conditions – no distractions.
  - **Review (1.5 hrs):** Score the MBE set. Thoroughly review explanations for all incorrect answers. Track your percentage correct overall and by subject – this is your first mini-benchmark.
- **Afternoon Block (e.g., 1:30 PM - 3:30 PM):**

    - **Weekly Review (2 hrs):** Review your notes from the entire week for both Torts and Contracts. Revisit areas that felt confusing. Solidify understanding of the basic rules covered.

- **Evening: REST.** Seriously. Take the evening off. Your brain needs downtime. Don't feel guilty ("I *should* be studying more!"). Rest is productive.

Day 7: Sunday

- **Option 1 (Catch-Up):** If you fell significantly behind during the week (missed a block, etc.), use 2-3 hours in the morning to catch up on the *most essential* missed task (likely practice questions or review). **Do not try to redo everything.**

- **Option 2 (Light Review & Planning):** If you're on track, use 1-2 hours to lightly review flashcards or notes from the week, and preview the schedule for Week 2.

- **Afternoon/Evening: REST and Recharge.** Do something non-law related. Prepare mentally for Week 2. Run errands, prepare food for the week – things that make the upcoming week smoother.

Weekend Structure Summary

Weekends in this schedule are not full days off (at least not initially). They serve specific purposes:

- **Longer Practice Blocks:** Simulate slightly longer periods of concentration (like the Saturday MBE set).

- **Review and Consolidation:** Dedicated time to review the week's material, helping move it from short-term to longer-term memory.

- **Catch-Up:** A buffer period for inevitable minor disruptions during the week. Use it wisely and sparingly.

- **Essential Rest:** Protected time off to prevent burnout and allow your brain to recover. Do not skip this! Demanding that you *must* study 24/7 is irrational and harmful.

Just Getting Started And Thats Okay

Week 1 is in the books. You survived! It likely felt like drinking from a firehose, and maybe your confidence took a few hits when you saw how many MBE questions you missed or how clunky your first attempts at IRAC felt. Excellent. That means you're engaging with the material and confronting reality. The irrationality lies in expecting this process to be easy or demanding instant perfection. You established a routine, you covered foundational material, you started practicing actively, and most importantly, you *kept going*. That's the win for this week. Don't awfulize about the difficulties; accept them as part of learning. Now, take a deep breath (a real one!), acknowledge the effort, and get ready to build on this foundation in Week 2.

Key Takeaways for Week 1

- Focus on establishing a consistent daily study routine and sticking to the schedule.
- Begin covering core concepts of foundational subjects (Torts, Contracts). Don't aim for immediate mastery; aim for familiarity and engagement.
- Incorporate active learning from Day 1: targeted MBE questions, untimed essay/MPT practice focusing on structure and format.
- Prioritize daily review of incorrect answers – this is where significant learning happens.
- Accept that feeling overwhelmed or making mistakes is normal, especially early on. Challenge perfectionistic demands ("I *must* understand this perfectly now!").
- Use the weekend for longer practice sets, consolidation review, limited catch-up, and essential rest.

Chapter 6: Week 2 - Expanding Core Knowledge

Alright, you laid the foundation in Week 1. You got into the rhythm (hopefully!), wrestled with Torts and Contracts, and started grappling with basic essay and MPT formats. Now, in Week 2, we expand. We introduce two more core MBE subjects – Real Property and Evidence – while continuing to reinforce Contracts. We also focus on refining that crucial essay structure (IRAC/CRAC). Expect challenges. Real Property, in particular, often makes people feel like their brains are leaking out of their ears (it's okay, that feeling is practically universal). Evidence involves lots of rules that seem designed purely to be confusing. You might feel frustrated, telling yourself, "This is impossible!" or "I'm just not smart enough for [Subject X]!" Recognize this as unhelpful self-talk. The rational approach is to acknowledge the difficulty, break down the material systematically (as the schedule helps you do), and persist with practice. Improvement comes from consistent effort, not from innate genius or lack thereof.

Weekly Overview

- **Goals for the Week:**
    - Maintain the daily study routine established in Week 1.
    - Cover core concepts of Real Property (Ownership Interests, Landlord-Tenant, Basic Conveyancing) and Evidence (Relevance, Character Evidence, Basic Hearsay). Continue solidifying Contracts (Defenses, Third-Party Rights - intro).
    - Complete approximately 200-225 targeted MBE questions across Real Property, Evidence, Contracts, and Torts (mixed review).
    - Refine IRAC application in essays; write one timed essay outline + untimed draft for Real Property and Evidence.
    - Practice analyzing and outlining a second MPT task (perhaps a persuasive brief format this time).
    - Continue daily review of incorrect answers, focusing on understanding the reasoning.
- **Subjects Covered:**

- MBE/Essays: Real Property (Present/Future Interests, Landlord-Tenant, Concurrent Estates, Easements intro), Evidence (Relevance, Character, Hearsay intro), Contracts (Defenses, Third-Party intro), Torts (Review).
- Skills: IRAC refinement, MPT format introduction (Persuasive Brief).

- **Key Tasks:**
  - Daily substantive review per schedule (approx. 1.5-2 hours/day).
  - Daily targeted/mixed MBE practice (approx. 30-35 questions/day).
  - Complete 1 timed outline/untimed draft essay for Real Property, 1 for Evidence.
  - Analyze and outline 1 MPT task (persuasive brief format).
  - Daily review of incorrect answers/model answers (approx. 1-1.5 hours/day).
- **Mindset Focus for the Week: Tolerating Frustration with Difficult Material**
  - You *will* encounter topics this week (hello, Rule Against Perpetuities!) that feel dense and confusing. The urge might be to avoid them, get angry ("This is stupid!"), or despair ("I'll *never* get this!"). These reactions, while common, are unproductive.
  - **Challenge:** Difficulty is not a sign of your inadequacy; it's a characteristic of the material. Frustration is a normal emotion when facing challenges, but it doesn't have to paralyze you.
  - **Rational Alternative:** "I accept that Real Property/Evidence is difficult and that I feel frustrated trying to learn it. However, feeling frustrated doesn't mean I *can't* learn it. My task is to break it down (following the schedule), practice applying the rules even if imperfectly, review my mistakes, and persist. Understanding will improve gradually with repeated exposure and effort. It doesn't *have* to feel easy."

Daily Schedule Day 1 - Day 7

(Maintain consistent timing as established in Week 1)

Day 1: Monday

- **Morning Block:**
  - **Substantive Review (1.5 hrs):** Real Property - Present Estates (Fee Simple, Defeasible Fees, Life Estate), Future Interests (Reversions, Remainders, Executory Interests – focus on basic identification). Brace yourself.
  - **MBE Practice (1.5 hrs):** 25-30 MBE questions on Real Property (Present/Future Interests). Don't panic if scores are low; this is notoriously hard. Focus on the explanations.
  - **Brief Review (30 mins):** Scan incorrect MBEs. Note the specific rules tested.
- **Afternoon Block:**
  - **Substantive Review (1.5 hrs):** Real Property - Concurrent Estates (Joint Tenancy, Tenancy in Common, Tenancy by Entirety), Landlord-Tenant Law (Types of Tenancies, Landlord/Tenant Duties - intro).
  - **MBE Practice (1 hr):** 15-20 MBE questions on Real Property (Concurrent Estates, Basic L-T).
  - **Essay Practice (1 hr):** Find a Real Property essay involving Present/Future Interests or Concurrent Estates. **Outline** the answer under timed conditions (10-15 mins). Then, write out the full essay **untimed**, focusing on applying IRAC correctly for each future interest or co-tenant issue.
- **Evening Block:**
  - **Review (1.5 hrs):** Thoroughly review incorrect MBEs (especially future interests!). Compare your RP essay outline/draft to the model. Where did your analysis differ? Consolidate RP notes.

Day 2: Tuesday

- **Morning Block:**
  - **Substantive Review (1.5 hrs):** Real Property - Landlord-Tenant Law (Assignment/Sublease, Eviction, Surrender), Easements (Creation, Scope, Termination - intro).

- **MBE Practice (1.5 hrs):** 25-30 MBE questions on Real Property (L-T issues, Easements).
- **Brief Review (30 mins):** Quick scan of incorrect MBE answers.

- **Afternoon Block:**
    - **Substantive Review (1.5 hrs):** Evidence - Introduction, Relevance (Logical & Legal Relevance - Rule 401, 403).
    - **MBE Practice (1 hr):** 15-20 MBE questions specifically on Evidence (Relevance). These often seem "easy" but have traps.
    - **Skills Practice (1 hr):** MPT Practice - Find a sample MPT asking for a Persuasive Brief. Read the Task Memo. Analyze the File and Library, focusing on identifying arguments for *your* client's side. What facts support you? What law supports you? How can you counter the opposition (if mentioned)? **Outline** the brief's argument sections.
- **Evening Block:**
    - **Review (1.5 hrs):** Review incorrect MBEs (RP & Evidence). Compare your MPT outline to the model answer's structure and arguments. Consolidate Evidence notes.

Day 3: Wednesday

- **Morning Block:**
    - **Substantive Review (1.5 hrs):** Evidence - Character Evidence (Civil vs. Criminal, Methods of Proof, Exceptions - MIMIC rules etc.). Complex area!
    - **MBE Practice (1.5 hrs):** 25-30 MBE questions on Evidence (Character Evidence). Expect difficulty matching the rule to the scenario.
    - **Brief Review (30 mins):** Quick scan of incorrect MBEs. Note character evidence exceptions.
- **Afternoon Block:**

- **Substantive Review (1.5 hrs):** Evidence - Basic Hearsay Analysis (Definition of Hearsay - Rule 801, intro to Non-Hearsay Exemptions - Opposing Party Statements, Prior Statements).
- **MBE Practice (1 hr):** 15-20 MBE questions on Evidence (Hearsay definition, basic exemptions).
- **Essay Practice (1 hr):** Find an Evidence essay involving Relevance and Character Evidence. **Outline** it timed (10-15 mins), then write the full essay **untimed**, carefully applying IRAC to each piece of evidence discussed.

- **Evening Block:**
  - **Review (1.5 hrs):** Thorough review of incorrect MBEs (Character & Hearsay!). Compare your Evidence essay to the model, focusing on rule statements and application. Consolidate Evidence notes.

Day 4: Thursday

- **Morning Block:**
  - **Substantive Review (1.5 hrs):** Contracts - Defenses to Formation Review (Mistake, Misrepresentation, etc.), Defenses to Enforcement (Illegality, Unconscionability, Statute of Frauds - overview).
  - **MBE Practice (1.5 hrs):** 25-30 MBE questions on Contracts (Defenses).
  - **Brief Review (30 mins):** Quick scan of incorrect MBEs.
- **Afternoon Block:**
  - **Substantive Review (1.5 hrs):** Contracts - Third-Party Rights (Intended/Incidental Beneficiaries, Assignment, Delegation - intro).
  - **MBE Practice (1 hr):** 15-20 MBE questions on Contracts (Third-Party Rights).
  - **MBE Review Practice (1 hr):** 20-25 **mixed** MBE questions covering Torts and Contracts (Week 1 material). This starts spaced repetition. Time yourself more strictly (~1.8 min/q).
- **Evening Block:**

- **Review (1.5 hrs):** Review incorrect MBEs from all sets today (Contracts Defenses, Third-Party, Torts/Contracts Review). Consolidate Contracts notes on Defenses/Third Parties.

Day 5: Friday

- **Morning Block:**
  - **Substantive Review (1.5 hrs):** Real Property - Review Weak Areas identified from Monday/Tuesday MBEs/Essay (e.g., Future Interests, L-T Duties).
  - **MBE Practice (1.5 hrs):** 30-35 mixed MBE questions on Real Property (covering all topics from the week). Time yourself strictly.
  - **Brief Review (30 mins):** Quick scan of incorrect MBEs.
- **Afternoon Block:**
  - **Substantive Review (1.5 hrs):** Evidence - Review Weak Areas identified from Wednesday MBEs/Essay (e.g., Character Evidence exceptions, Hearsay definition).
  - **MBE Practice (1 hr):** 25-30 mixed MBE questions on Evidence (covering all topics from the week). Time yourself strictly.
  - **MPT Practice (1 hr):** Look back at the Persuasive Brief MPT task. Review your outline from Tuesday. Try to write out **one full argument section** (e.g., the first major point) based on your outline, focusing on weaving together facts from the File and rules from the Library to support your client's position.
- **Evening Block:**
  - **Review (1.5 hrs):** Thorough review of incorrect MBEs (RP & Evidence mix). Compare your written MPT section to the corresponding section in the model answer. How effectively did you argue?

Day 6: Saturday

- **Morning Block (e.g., 9:00 AM - 1:00 PM):**

- **Mixed MBE Practice (3 hrs):** 100 MBE questions, timed (3 hours). Mix of Torts, Contracts, Real Property, Evidence. Simulate a full morning MBE session. No distractions.
- **Review (1 hr):** Score the MBE set. Calculate overall percentage and percentage by subject. **Do not review explanations yet** - save that for the afternoon block. Take a break.

- **Afternoon Block (e.g., 2:00 PM - 5:00 PM):**
    - **MBE Explanation Review (3 hrs):** This is intense but necessary. Go through the explanations for *all* 100 questions, focusing on the incorrect ones but also reinforcing why you got the right ones right. Note weak areas that persist.
- **Evening: REST.** You've earned it after that MBE session. Get away from the books.

Day 7: Sunday

- **Option 1 (Targeted Review/Catch-Up):** Use 2-3 hours to review notes or do extra practice questions specifically on the subjects/topics you performed worst on during the Saturday MBE set. Or catch up on any essential task missed during the week.
- **Option 2 (Essay/MPT Skill Refinement):** Use 1-2 hours to review IRAC structure using model answers, or practice outlining another MPT.
- **Afternoon/Evening: REST and Recharge.** Plan for Week 3. Prepare mentally for new subjects and increasing integration.

Weekend Structure Summary

The weekend structure intensifies slightly in Week 2, particularly with the longer 100-question timed MBE session on Saturday. This serves several purposes:

- **Building Endurance:** Getting used to sustained focus for a 3-hour block.
- **Integrated Practice:** Testing your ability to switch between subjects under pressure.

- **Assessment:** Providing a larger data set to assess your progress and identify weak areas across multiple subjects.
- **Dedicated Review:** Allocating significant time (Saturday afternoon) to digest the feedback from the longer practice set.
- **Continued Rest:** Sunday remains crucial for recovery and preventing burnout.

Pressing On Through the Fog

Week 2 often feels like wading through intellectual mud – Real Property and Evidence can do that. You might have felt more frustration this week than last. Good. Tolerating that frustration, sticking to the schedule *despite* the difficulty, and continuing to practice actively is precisely the mental toughness you need. You covered more ground, started mixing subjects in practice, and hopefully felt your essay structuring become slightly less awkward. Don't demand clarity on every single point yet; that's irrational. Acknowledge the effort, accept the persistent fog in some areas (it will lift, slowly, with more repetition), and recognize that you are making progress simply by *doing the work*. Week 3 will bring new challenges and further integration. Keep going.

Key Takeaways for Week 2

- Persist with the daily routine even when facing difficult subjects like Real Property and Evidence.
- Actively work on refining IRAC application in essays, moving towards outlining under timed conditions.
- Begin incorporating mixed MBE review questions to practice subject switching and reinforce earlier material (spaced repetition).
- Practice analyzing and outlining different MPT task formats (e.g., persuasive brief).
- Accept frustration with difficult topics as normal; challenge catastrophic thinking ("I'll *never* get this!") and focus on persistent, structured effort.
- Use longer weekend practice sets (like the 100 MBE questions) to build endurance and get better assessment data, followed by thorough review.

- Prioritize daily review and weekend rest to consolidate learning and prevent burnout.

Okay, you’ve navigated the initial foundational weeks. You’ve wrestled with core subjects, started getting the hang of the routine (even if it feels like wrestling a greased pig sometimes), and begun building essential skills. Now, as we enter Week 3, the focus shifts towards **integration**. We’re adding more hefty MBE subjects – Criminal Law, Criminal Procedure, and Civil Procedure – and you'll start seeing more mixed practice. The goal isn't just to learn these subjects in isolation but to begin weaving them together with what you already know. You might feel your brain starting to short-circuit, thinking, "How can I possibly hold all these rules simultaneously?!" That's a common, though unhelpful, thought. The reality is, law isn't neatly compartmentalized; rules overlap and interact. This week starts training your brain to make those connections, which is crucial for both MBE and essay performance. Expect some mental friction – it’s a sign that learning is happening.

Chapter 7: Week 3 - Integrating Concepts

This week introduces Criminal Law, Criminal Procedure, and the often-dreaded Civil Procedure. These subjects are rule-heavy and frequently tested. Simultaneously, we'll increase the mixing of subjects in your MBE practice and introduce more strictly timed sets. The aim is to build your capacity to recall and apply rules across different legal areas under time pressure. Don't demand instant recall or perfect scores on timed sets – that's setting yourself up for unnecessary grief. Focus on executing the daily plan, engaging actively with the new material, practicing the integration through mixed sets, and diligently reviewing your mistakes.

Weekly Overview

- **Goals for the Week:**
  - Maintain consistent daily study routine.
  - Cover core concepts of Criminal Law (Homicide, Other Crimes, Accomplice Liability, Defenses), Criminal Procedure (4th, 5th, 6th Amendment issues), and Civil Procedure (Jurisdiction, Venue, Erie, Pleadings).
  - Complete approximately 225-250 MBE questions, with an increasing proportion in timed, mixed sets covering all subjects learned to date.
  - Practice IRAC on Criminal Law/Procedure and Civil Procedure essays (timed outline/untimed writing).
  - Attempt writing a short section of an MPT under timed conditions.
  - Continue rigorous daily review of incorrect answers, noting cross-subject connections (e.g., evidence rules in a criminal context).
- **Subjects Covered:**
  - MBE/Essays: Criminal Law, Criminal Procedure, Civil Procedure (Jurisdiction, Venue, Erie, Pleadings).
  - Review: Torts, Contracts, Real Property, Evidence.
  - Skills: Essay practice (IRAC), MPT timed writing snippet, Timed MBE set practice.

- **Key Tasks:**
  - Daily substantive review per schedule (approx. 1.5-2 hours/day).
  - Daily targeted MBE practice + introduction of timed mixed MBE sets (approx. 35-40 questions/day total).
  - Complete 1 timed outline/untimed draft essay for Crim Law/Pro, 1 for Civ Pro.
  - Attempt writing one MPT section timed (e.g., 20-30 mins for one argument).
  - Daily review of incorrect answers/model answers (approx. 1.5 hours/day).
- **Mindset Focus for the Week: Embracing Integration, Tolerating Ambiguity**
  - As subjects pile up, you might desperately want to keep them in neat, separate boxes in your head ("I *must* master Crim Law before I mix it with Torts!"). This isn't how the exam (or law) works. You'll see MBE questions blending concepts; essays often hit multiple subjects.
  - **Challenge:** Resisting integration increases anxiety. Demanding perfect clarity before mixing subjects is unrealistic.
  - **Rational Alternative:** "I accept that legal issues often overlap and that practicing integration now, even if confusing, will help me on the actual exam. It's okay if I don't feel 100% confident in Crim Law before doing mixed MBE sets. The mixing *itself* is part of the learning process. I can tolerate the initial ambiguity and trust that connections will become clearer with repeated practice and review."

Daily Schedule Day 1 - Day 7

(Maintain consistent timing)

Day 1: Monday

- **Morning Block:**
  - **Substantive Review (1.5 hrs):** Criminal Law - Homicide (Common Law Murder, degrees, Voluntary/Involuntary Manslaughter).

- MBE Practice (1.5 hrs): 25-30 MBE questions specifically on Criminal Law (Homicide).
    - **Brief Review (30 mins):** Scan incorrect MBEs. Note elements of different homicide types.
- **Afternoon Block:**
    - **Substantive Review (1.5 hrs):** Criminal Law - Other Crimes Against the Person (Battery, Assault, Kidnapping), Property Crimes (Larceny, Embezzlement, False Pretenses, Robbery, Burglary).
    - **MBE Practice (1 hr):** 15-20 MBE questions on Criminal Law (Other Crimes).
    - **Essay Practice (1 hr):** Find a Criminal Law essay covering Homicide or Property Crimes. **Outline** it timed (10-15 mins), then write the full essay **untimed**, applying IRAC rigorously.
- **Evening Block:**
    - **Review (1.5 hrs):** Thoroughly review incorrect MBEs. Compare your Crim Law essay to the model. Consolidate Crim Law notes.

Day 2: Tuesday

- **Morning Block:**
    - **Substantive Review (1.5 hrs):** Criminal Law - Accomplice Liability, Inchoate Offenses (Solicitation, Conspiracy, Attempt), Defenses (Insanity, Intoxication, Infancy, Self-Defense, Duress, Necessity).
    - **MBE Practice (1.5 hrs):** 25-30 MBE questions on Criminal Law (Accomplice, Inchoate, Defenses).
    - **Brief Review (30 mins):** Quick scan of incorrect MBE answers.
- **Afternoon Block:**
    - **Substantive Review (1 hr):** Criminal Procedure - Introduction, 4th Amendment: Search & Seizure (Government Action, Standing/REP, Warrants, Exceptions intro).

- **Timed Mixed MBE Set (1.5 hrs):** 35-40 MBE questions, **timed** (approx. 1.8 min/q). Mix should include Crim Law (from Mon/Tues) + Torts, Contracts, Real Property, Evidence. **Simulate test conditions.**
- **Brief Review (30 mins):** Score the timed set. Quickly identify subjects you struggled with most *under pressure*. Deeper review tonight.

- **Evening Block:**
  - **Review (1.5 hrs):** Thorough review of incorrect MBEs from *both* the morning Crim Law set and the afternoon timed mixed set. Focus on *why* you missed questions under timing pressure. Start Crim Pro notes.

Day 3: Wednesday

- **Morning Block:**
  - **Substantive Review (1.5 hrs):** Criminal Procedure - 4th Amdt Search & Seizure Exceptions (Plain View, Consent, Search Incident to Arrest, Auto, Exigent Circumstances, Stop & Frisk). Exclusionary Rule & Fruit of Poisonous Tree.
  - **MBE Practice (1.5 hrs):** 25-30 MBE questions on Criminal Procedure (Search & Seizure). These are often fact-intensive.
  - **Brief Review (30 mins):** Quick scan of incorrect MBEs. Note requirements for key exceptions.
- **Afternoon Block:**
  - **Substantive Review (1 hr):** Criminal Procedure - 5th Amendment (Miranda Rights, Double Jeopardy, Privilege Against Self-Incrimination).
  - **Essay Practice (1.5 hrs):** Find a Criminal Procedure essay (likely focusing on 4th or 5th Amdt issues). **Outline** timed (10-15 mins). Write full essay **untimed**, applying IRAC. Pay attention to how facts trigger specific rules/exceptions.
  - **Skills Practice (30 mins):** MPT Timed Writing - Take the MPT outline you did last week (or a section of today's essay outline). Try to write out just *one* complete paragraph or argument section within a strict time

limit (e.g., 10-15 minutes). Get used to writing concise analysis under pressure.

- **Evening Block:**
    - **Review (1.5 hrs):** Thorough review of incorrect MBEs. Compare Crim Pro essay to model. Review your timed MPT writing snippet – was it coherent? Did you hit key points quickly? Consolidate Crim Pro notes.

Day 4: Thursday

- **Morning Block:**
    - **Substantive Review (1.5 hrs):** Criminal Procedure - 6th Amendment (Right to Counsel, Confrontation Clause, Speedy Trial, Jury Trial). 8th Amendment (Cruel & Unusual Punishment - intro).
    - **MBE Practice (1.5 hrs):** 25-30 MBE questions on Criminal Procedure (5th, 6th, 8th Amdt issues).[1]
    - **Brief Review (30 mins):** Quick scan of incorrect MBEs.
- **Afternoon Block:**
    - **Substantive Review (1 hr):** Civil Procedure - Subject Matter Jurisdiction (Federal Question, Diversity, Supplemental).
    - **Timed Mixed MBE Set (1.5 hrs):** 35-40 MBE questions, **timed**. Mix covering all subjects so far (Torts, K, RP, Evid, Crim L, Crim Pro).
    - **Brief Review (30 mins):** Score the timed set. Note patterns in errors under pressure.
- **Evening Block:**
    - **Review (1.5 hrs):** Thorough review of incorrect MBEs from both sets. Start Civ Pro notes (SMJ).

Day 5: Friday

- **Morning Block:**

- **Substantive Review (1.5 hrs):** Civil Procedure - Personal Jurisdiction (Constitutional Limits, Long-Arm Statutes, Consent/Waiver, In Rem/Quasi In Rem). Venue.
- **MBE Practice (1.5 hrs):** 25-30 MBE questions on Civil Procedure (PJ, Venue). These often require careful step-by-step analysis.
- **Brief Review (30 mins):** Quick scan of incorrect MBEs.

- **Afternoon Block:**
  - **Substantive Review (1 hr):** Civil Procedure - Erie Doctrine. Pleadings (Complaint, Rule 12 Motions, Answer).
  - **MBE Practice (1 hr):** 15-20 MBE questions on Civil Procedure (Erie, Pleadings).
  - **Essay Practice (1 hr):** Find a Civil Procedure essay (likely on Jurisdiction or Erie). **Outline** timed (10-15 mins). Write full essay **untimed**, applying IRAC methodically.
- **Evening Block:**
  - **Review (1.5 hrs):** Thorough review of incorrect MBEs. Compare Civ Pro essay to model. Consolidate Civ Pro notes.

Day 6: Saturday

- **Morning Block (e.g., 9:00 AM - 1:00 PM):**
  - **Timed Mixed MBE Practice (3 hrs):** 100 MBE questions, timed (3 hours). Mix covering all 7 MBE subjects studied so far. Full simulation.
  - **Review (1 hr):** Score the MBE set. Calculate overall % and % by subject. Note immediate reactions/areas of perceived weakness. Take a break before deep review.
- **Afternoon Block (e.g., 2:00 PM - 5:00 PM):**
  - **MBE Explanation Review (3 hrs):** Rigorous review of explanations for the 100-question set. Focus on incorrect answers but understand the right ones too. Where are errors concentrated? Are they rule gaps or application errors?

- **Evening: REST.** Absolutely essential after that mental workout.

Day 7: Sunday

- **Option 1 (Targeted Review/Catch-Up):** Use 2-3 hours focusing on the 1-2 subjects you performed worst on during Saturday's MBE set. Do targeted practice questions or review notes specifically for those areas. Or catch up if needed.
- **Option 2 (Essay/MPT Skills):** Use 1-2 hours to review IRAC structure across different subjects, or attempt outlining another MPT focusing on structure and timing the outline portion.
- **Afternoon/Evening: REST and Recharge.** Prepare for Week 4 – the halfway point!

Weekend Structure Summary

Week 3 maintains the weekend structure from Week 2, solidifying the routine of a long, timed, mixed MBE set on Saturday followed by deep review. This integrated practice is critical now that all seven core MBE subjects have been introduced. Sunday remains flexible for targeted work based on Saturday's results, alongside crucial rest. Don't underestimate the cumulative fatigue; proper rest is not optional.

Juggling More Balls Without Dropping Them All

You've now been introduced to all seven MBE subjects. Congratulations – that's a significant milestone! It probably feels like you're juggling way too many balls, and some feel slippery (Civil Procedure, anyone?). That's okay. The introduction of timed mixed MBE sets this week likely added another layer of pressure. The key takeaway is not that you *must* juggle perfectly right now, but that you *started practicing the juggling*. You forced your brain to switch contexts, to pull rules from different areas, sometimes under time pressure. This skill improves only with practice. Accept the initial clumsiness, keep following the schedule, review diligently, and trust that the repetition and integration built into the plan will gradually improve your ability to keep those balls in the air. You're building capacity. Now, let's head towards the midpoint.

Key Takeaways for Week 3

- Successfully introduced Criminal Law, Criminal Procedure, and Civil Procedure into the study mix.
- Began practicing integration through increasingly frequent timed, mixed MBE sets covering all subjects learned.
- Continued applying and refining IRAC structure in essays for the newly introduced subjects.
- Started experimenting with timed writing for small MPT sections or essay outlines.
- Practiced tolerating the ambiguity and confusion that comes with learning complex, overlapping subjects, challenging demands for instant clarity.
- Maintained the routine of significant weekend practice (100 timed MBEs) followed by thorough review and essential rest.

Chapter 8: Week 4 - Midpoint Check-in & MEE Subjects

Here we are at Week 4, the halfway point of this 8-week sprint. Pause for a second and acknowledge that: you've put in three solid weeks of intense work. That's something. This week, we introduce Constitutional Law – another MBE heavyweight – and the first major MEE-focused subject block, Business Associations. We also dedicate specific time to MPT strategy, particularly timing. Critically, the end of this week includes a **midpoint check-in**: a time to objectively assess your progress against the goals you set back in Chapter 3. Don't let the halfway mark trigger panic ("Only four weeks left! I'm doomed!") or complacency ("I'm halfway, I can relax!"). Use it as a rational opportunity to evaluate where you are, adjust your focus for the second half if needed, and reaffirm your commitment to the process.

Weekly Overview

- **Goals for the Week:**
    - Cover core concepts of Constitutional Law (Judicial Review, Separation of Powers, Federalism, Dormant Commerce Clause, Individual Rights - focus on Equal Protection, Substantive/Procedural Due Process, 1st Amdt Speech).
    - Cover core concepts of Business Associations (Agency, Partnerships, Corporations formation/liability/duties).
    - Complete approximately 225-250 MBE questions, continuing timed mixed sets.
    - Practice IRAC essays on Con Law and Bus Ass (timed outline/untimed writing).
    - Learn and practice a specific MPT timing strategy (e.g., 45 min read/outline, 45 min write). Attempt one full MPT under timed conditions using the strategy.
    - Conduct a midpoint check-in: review progress on goals, analyze performance data, identify persistent weak areas.
- **Subjects Covered:**

- MBE/MEE: Constitutional Law, Business Associations (Agency, Partnerships, Corporations).[2]
- Review: All previous MBE subjects.
- Skills: Essay practice (IRAC), MPT Timing Strategy & Timed Practice, Midpoint Assessment.

- **Key Tasks:**
    - Daily substantive review per schedule (approx. 1.5-2 hours/day).
    - Daily targeted/mixed MBE practice (approx. 35-40 questions/day).
    - Complete 1 timed outline/untimed draft essay for Con Law, 1 for Bus Ass.
    - Complete 1 full MPT under timed conditions using a specific timing strategy.
    - Perform midpoint assessment (review diagnostic vs. current scores, identify weak areas).
    - Daily review of incorrect answers/model answers (approx. 1.5 hours/day).
- **Mindset Focus for the Week: Objective Assessment Over Emotional Reaction**
    - Reaching the midpoint can trigger strong emotions – anxiety about time running out, frustration with slow progress, maybe even despair. You might tell yourself, "I *should* be scoring much higher by now!" or "Compared to [some mythical perfect student], I'm so far behind!"
    - **Challenge:** Basing your assessment purely on feelings or comparisons is irrational and unhelpful. Feelings are not facts. Comparisons are usually based on incomplete or distorted information.
    - **Rational Alternative:** "My feelings of anxiety are understandable, but they don't accurately reflect my progress. I will look at the **objective data**: my practice scores (diagnostic vs. now), the number of practice questions/essays completed, my adherence to the schedule. Based on this *evidence*, I will assess my strengths and weaknesses and rationally

decide if any adjustments are needed for the next four weeks. I accept my current position without demanding it *should* be different."

Daily Schedule Day 1 - Day 7

(Maintain consistent timing)

Day 1: Monday

- **Morning Block:**
    - **Substantive Review (1.5 hrs):** Constitutional Law - Judicial Review (Standing, Ripeness, Mootness, Political Question), Separation of Powers, Federalism principles.
    - **MBE Practice (1.5 hrs):** 25-30 MBE questions specifically on Constitutional Law (Justiciability, Powers).
    - **Brief Review (30 mins):** Scan incorrect MBEs. Note key justiciability requirements.
- **Afternoon Block:**
    - **Substantive Review (1.5 hrs):** Constitutional Law - Dormant Commerce Clause, State Action Doctrine, Procedural Due Process.
    - **MBE Practice (1 hr):** 15-20 MBE questions on Constitutional Law (DCC, State Action, PDP).
    - **Essay Practice (1 hr):** Find a Constitutional Law essay (perhaps on Standing or Federalism). **Outline** timed (10-15 mins). Write full essay **untimed**, applying IRAC.
- **Evening Block:**
    - **Review (1.5 hrs):** Thoroughly review incorrect MBEs. Compare Con Law essay to model. Start Con Law notes.

Day 2: Tuesday

- **Morning Block:**

- **Substantive Review (1.5 hrs):** Constitutional Law - Substantive Due Process (Fundamental Rights), Equal Protection (Classifications, Levels of Scrutiny). Dense material!
- **MBE Practice (1.5 hrs):** 25-30 MBE questions on Constitutional Law (SDP, EP). Expect careful fact analysis is needed.
- **Brief Review (30 mins):** Quick scan of incorrect MBE answers. Note triggers for different scrutiny levels.

- **Afternoon Block:**
  - **Substantive Review (1 hr):** Constitutional Law - First Amendment: Free Speech (Content-based vs. Content-neutral, Unprotected Categories, Time/Place/Manner).
  - **Timed Mixed MBE Set (1.5 hrs):** 35-40 MBE questions, **timed**. Mix covering all MBE subjects including Con Law foundations.
  - **Brief Review (30 mins):** Score the timed set. Note error patterns.
- **Evening Block:**
  - **Review (1.5 hrs):** Thorough review of incorrect MBEs from both sets (Con Law specifics, Mixed set). Consolidate Con Law notes.

Day 3: Wednesday

- **Morning Block:**
  - **Substantive Review (1.5 hrs):** Business Associations - Agency (Creation of Agency Relationship, Authority - Actual/Apparent, Agent's Duties, Liability of Principal/Agent).
  - **MEE Subject MBE?** (Check your Q-bank: some platforms include Bus Ass questions, others don't. If available, do 20-25 Qs. If not, substitute with mixed MBE review).
  - **Brief Review (30 mins):** Scan incorrect MBEs or review Agency rules.
- **Afternoon Block:**

    - **Substantive Review (1.5 hrs):** Business Associations - Partnerships (Formation, Liability, Fiduciary Duties, Dissociation/Dissolution).
    - **(MBE Practice - if available, 15-20 Qs on Partnerships. If not, skip or do mixed MBE).**
    - **Essay Practice (1 hr+):** Find a Business Associations essay (Agency or Partnership focus). **Outline** timed (10-15 mins). Write full essay **untimed**, applying IRAC to agency authority or partnership liability issues.
- **Evening Block:**
    - **Review (1.5 hrs):** Review incorrect MBEs (if any). Compare Bus Ass essay carefully to model answer. Start Bus Ass notes.

Day 4: Thursday

- **Morning Block:**
    - **Substantive Review (1.5 hrs):** Business Associations - Corporations (Formation, Piercing the Corporate Veil, Pre-Incorporation Contracts, Basic Stock concepts).
    - **(MBE Practice - if available, 20-25 Qs on Corp Formation/PCV. If not, use mixed MBE).**
    - **Brief Review (30 mins):** Scan incorrect MBEs or review Corp formation rules.
- **Afternoon Block:**
    - **Substantive Review (1.5 hrs):** Business Associations - Corporations (Directors' & Officers' Duties - Duty of Care, Duty of Loyalty).
    - **(MBE Practice - if available, 15-20 Qs on D&O Duties. If not, use mixed MBE).**
    - **Essay Practice (1 hr+):** Find a Corporations essay (PCV or D&O Duties). **Outline** timed (10-15 mins). Write full essay **untimed**, applying IRAC.
- **Evening Block:**

- **Review (1.5 hrs):** Review incorrect MBEs. Compare Corporations essay to model. Consolidate Bus Ass notes.

Day 5: Friday - MPT Strategy & Practice

- **Morning Block:**
  - **Skills Focus (1.5 hrs): MPT Timing Strategy.** Read this section carefully: A highly recommended approach is the **45/45 split**.
    - **First 45 Minutes (Read, Analyze, Outline):**
      - (5 min) Read Task Memo carefully. Understand your role, the requested document, audience, tone (objective/persuasive).
      - (5-10 min) Skim File & Library headings/structure. Get the lay of the land.
      - (25-30 min) Read File & Library *actively*. Highlight key facts, relevant rules, potential counterarguments. Start formulating your structure/arguments. **Create a working outline** as you go or immediately after reading. This outline is your roadmap for writing. **Do NOT skip the outline!** Thinking you can just start writing without a plan under pressure is foolish.
    - **Second 45 Minutes (Write):**
      - Write the document based *directly* on your outline. Focus on clear structure (use headings!), concise rule statements, and applying key facts to the rules.
      - Follow formatting instructions precisely. Allocate time within this block (e.g., Intro/Conclusion 5 min, Argument 1 15 min, Argument 2 15 min, Polish 5 min).
      - **Goal:** Get a structurally sound, responsive document written. It won't be perfect, but it needs to be complete and follow instructions. Practice helps you internalize this timing.

    - **Mixed MBE Practice (1.5 hrs):** 30-35 **timed** MBE questions, mixed subjects.
    - **Brief Review (30 mins):** Review incorrect MBEs.
- **Afternoon Block (e.g., 1:30 PM - 3:00 PM):**
    - **Timed MPT Practice (1.5 hrs):** Take one full MPT. Apply the 45/45 timing strategy (or adjust slightly if needed, e.g., 50/40, but have a plan!). **Stick to the time.** Stop writing when time is up.
- **Later Afternoon (e.g., 3:30 PM - 5:00 PM):**
    - **MPT Review (1.5 hrs):** Compare your timed MPT answer to the model answer and point sheet. Did you follow the Task Memo? Did you use key facts/rules? Was your structure logical? How did the timing strategy work for you? Where did you run out of time? Be honest.
- **Evening Block:**
    - **Light Review / REST (1.5 hrs):** Review notes from the week or simply take an extended break. You did a full timed MPT today!

Day 6: Saturday - Midpoint Check-in & Practice

- **Morning Block (e.g., 9:00 AM - 12:30 PM):**
    - **Practice Simulation (Approx. 3 hrs):** Choose one:
        - Option A: 100 Timed Mixed MBE questions (3 hours).
        - Option B: 2-3 Timed Essays (e.g., 1 Con Law, 1 Bus Ass, 1 older subject) (1-1.5 hours) + 50 Timed Mixed MBE questions (1.5 hours).
        - Option C: 1 Timed MPT (if you didn't do one Friday or want more practice) (1.5 hours) + 50 Timed Mixed MBE questions (1.5 hours).
    - **Scoring/Initial Impressions (30 mins):** Score your work. Note initial thoughts on performance. Take a break.
- **Afternoon Block (e.g., 1:30 PM - 5:00 PM):**

- **Midpoint Assessment & Review (3.5 hrs):**
    - **(1.5 hrs) Review Practice:** Thoroughly review explanations/model answers from the morning's practice simulation.
    - **(2 hrs) Check-in:**
        - **Gather Data:** Pull out your Chapter 3 diagnostic scores and goals. Look at your scores from today (and previous weekend sets).
        - **Analyze:** Compare diagnostic to current performance. By subject? By skill (MBE, Essay, MPT)? Are you on track with your SMART goals? Where are the biggest persistent weaknesses? Where have you improved most? **Be objective.** Don't let feelings ("I *feel* like I know nothing!") override the data.
        - **Adjust?:** Based *only* on the data, do you need to adjust your focus for Weeks 5-8? E.g., if MPT scores are still very low, maybe swap one essay practice slot per week for an MPT slot? If one MBE subject is dragging everything down, plan to dedicate slightly more review time to it during scheduled review blocks? Make *small, rational* adjustments if needed. Don't overhaul the whole plan based on anxiety. Write down any adjustments.

- **Evening: REST.** Midpoint assessment can be draining.

Day 7: Sunday

- **Review/Planning (1-2 hours):** Lightly review notes from your weakest areas identified during the check-in. Look ahead at the schedule for Week 5 (more MEE subjects, more timed practice). Prepare mentally.
- **Afternoon/Evening: REST and Recharge.** Acknowledge completing half the program. Prepare logistically for the upcoming week.

Weekend Structure Summary

Week 4's weekend is pivotal. Saturday includes a significant practice block followed by dedicated time for **objective midpoint assessment**. This isn't just about reviewing answers; it's about strategically evaluating progress against initial goals and making rational, data-driven adjustments to the plan for the second half if necessary. Sunday remains focused on targeted review based on the assessment and essential rest before plunging into the latter half of the schedule.

Taking Stock Without Taking Fright

The halfway point. It's easy to get spooked here, focusing only on the time remaining or perceived shortcomings. But you just navigated Con Law and Business Associations, tackled timed MPT strategy, and—most importantly—you performed an objective check-in. Looking at data, even if it's not exactly what you hoped for, is far more productive than wallowing in vague anxiety. You have information now. You know where to apply pressure in the coming weeks. Accept the data, make rational adjustments if needed, and refuse to engage in catastrophic thinking about the remaining time. You have four more weeks of structured work ahead. Use the information from your assessment to make them count. Onward to Week 5.

Key Takeaways for Week 4

- Introduced and covered core concepts of Constitutional Law and Business Associations.
- Dedicated specific time to learning and practicing an MPT timing strategy (e.g., 45/45 split) and completed a fully timed MPT.
- Continued integrating subjects through timed mixed MBE sets.
- Conducted a crucial midpoint check-in: objectively compared current performance data against diagnostic scores and goals.
- Used assessment data to identify persistent weak areas and make rational, minor adjustments to the study plan for Weeks 5-8 if necessary.
- Practiced objective self-assessment, challenging emotional reactions and comparisons unsupported by evidence.

- Maintained focus on consistent practice, review, and rest despite midpoint fatigue or anxiety.

Chapter 9: Week 5 - Ramping Up Practice

You've crossed the midpoint. You have assessed your progress, identified lingering weaknesses, and perhaps made some minor adjustments to your focus. Now, in Week 5, we continue to broaden our subject knowledge by adding two more common MEE subjects – Family Law and Wills & Estates – while significantly **ramping up the intensity and frequency of timed practice** across all components. Expect more timed MBE sets, a greater emphasis on writing full essays within the 30-minute window, and continued timed MPT practice. The goal is to build not just knowledge, but also speed and efficiency under pressure. You might feel spread thin with the addition of new subjects alongside the push for speed. The irrational thought "I can't possibly cover everything *and* go faster!" might surface. Counter it by trusting the process: consistent, timed practice, even if imperfect, builds the necessary skills. Focus on execution, not on demanding simultaneous perfection and speed.

Weekly Overview

- **Goals for the Week:**
    - Cover core concepts of Family Law (Marriage requirements/dissolution, Property Division, Child Custody/Support) and Wills & Estates (Intestacy, Will Formation/Revocation/Contests, Basic Trust Introduction).
    - Complete approximately 250+ MBE questions, primarily in timed mixed sets covering all 7 MBE subjects.
    - Increase frequency of timed essay practice, aiming to write at least 2-3 full essays within the 30-minute limit.
    - Attempt another MPT under fully timed conditions, reinforcing the timing strategy.
    - Continue rigorous daily review, focusing on both rule understanding and application speed.
- **Subjects Covered:**
    - MEE: Family Law, Wills & Estates.

- Review: All 7 MBE subjects + Business Associations (integrated into practice).
- Skills: Increased Timed Essay Writing, Timed MPT Practice, Timed Mixed MBE Sets.

- **Key Tasks:**
  - Daily substantive review of new MEE subjects + targeted review of weak MBE areas (approx. 1.5-2 hours/day).
  - Daily timed mixed MBE practice (sets of 30-50 questions) (approx. 1.5-2 hours/day).
  - Complete 2-3 fully timed essays (30 mins each) covering a mix of subjects.
  - Complete 1 fully timed MPT (90 mins).
  - Daily review of incorrect answers/model answers (approx. 1.5-2 hours/day).
- **Mindset Focus for the Week: Building Speed Through Persistent Practice**
  - The push for timed practice can trigger anxiety: "I can't think/write that fast!" "My score drops when I time myself!" "I *must* write perfect answers, even timed!" This is normal but unhelpful. Speed doesn't come from magic; it comes from familiarity and repetition.
  - **Challenge:** Demanding perfection under time pressure leads to freezing or sloppy work. Focusing solely on low timed scores breeds discouragement.
  - **Rational Alternative:** "I accept that writing timed answers is challenging and my first attempts might be messy or incomplete. My goal isn't immediate perfection, but *practice*. Each timed drill helps me internalize the pacing, identify essential points quicker, and write more concisely. My speed and accuracy will improve *gradually* with consistent, deliberate timed practice and review. I focus on the process, not just the initial scores."

Daily Schedule Day 1 - Day 7

(Shift towards more timed practice, especially in afternoon blocks)

Day 1: Monday

- **Morning Block:**
  - **Substantive Review (1.5 hrs):** Family Law - Marriage (Formal requirements, Common Law Marriage), Annulment, Divorce (Jurisdiction, Grounds), Separation Agreements.
  - **Timed Mixed MBE Set (1.5 hrs):** 40-50 MBE questions, **timed**. Mix of all 7 MBE subjects.
  - **Brief Review (30 mins):** Score MBE set. Quickly review explanations for 5-10 incorrect answers, focusing on *why* you missed them. Deeper review later.
- **Afternoon Block:**
  - **Substantive Review (1 hr):** Family Law - Division of Property (Separate vs. Marital Property, Equitable Distribution/Community Property basics), Spousal Support (Alimony).
  - **Timed Essay Practice (1 hr):** Find a Family Law essay (e.g., on property division or spousal support). **Write the full essay under timed conditions (30 minutes).** Stop when time is up, even if unfinished.
  - **Essay Self-Critique (30 mins):** Immediately after, compare your timed essay to the model answer. How much did you cover? Was your IRAC clear? Where did time run out?
  - **(Optional Extra MBE: 30 mins - 15-20 Qs targeted on weak area identified last week).**
- **Evening Block:**
  - **Review (1.5 hrs):** Thorough review of incorrect MBEs from morning set. Deeper review of timed Family Law essay against model. Start Family Law notes.

Day 2: Tuesday

- **Morning Block:**

- **Substantive Review (1.5 hrs):** Family Law - Child Custody (Jurisdiction - UCCJEA, Best Interests of the Child standard), Child Support (Guidelines, Modification, Enforcement).
- **Timed Mixed MBE Set (1.5 hrs):** 40-50 MBE questions, **timed**. Mix of all 7 MBE subjects.
- **Brief Review (30 mins):** Score MBE set. Quick review of 5-10 incorrects.

- **Afternoon Block:**
  - **Targeted MBE Review/Practice (1 hr):** Focus on your 1-2 weakest MBE subjects identified during Week 4 check-in. Review notes briefly, then do 25-30 **timed** questions *only* on that subject.
  - **Timed Essay Practice (1 hr):** Find an essay on a subject you find difficult (e.g., Real Property, Con Law). **Write the full essay under timed conditions (30 minutes).**
  - **Essay Self-Critique (30 mins):** Compare timed essay to model answer. Focus on issue spotting and analysis under pressure.
- **Evening Block:**
  - **Review (1.5 hrs):** Thorough review of incorrect MBEs (morning mixed set + afternoon targeted set). Deeper review of timed essay. Consolidate Family Law notes.

Day 3: Wednesday

- **Morning Block:**
  - **Substantive Review (1.5 hrs):** Wills & Estates - Intestate Succession, Will Formation Requirements (Capacity, Formalities - execution, witnesses).
  - **Timed Mixed MBE Set (1.5 hrs):** 40-50 MBE questions, **timed**. Mix of all 7 MBE subjects.
  - **Brief Review (30 mins):** Score MBE set. Quick review of 5-10 incorrects.
- **Afternoon Block:**

- **Substantive Review (1 hr):** Wills & Estates - Will Revocation (By physical act, subsequent instrument, operation of law), Will Contests (Lack of capacity, undue influence, fraud).
- **Timed Essay Practice (1 hr):** Find a Wills essay (e.g., on will validity or revocation). **Write the full essay under timed conditions (30 minutes).**
- **Essay Self-Critique (30 mins):** Compare timed essay to model answer. Did you hit the key requirements/elements for validity or revocation?

- **Evening Block:**
  - **Review (1.5 hrs):** Thorough review of incorrect MBEs. Deeper review of timed Wills essay. Start Wills & Estates notes.

Day 4: Thursday

- **Morning Block:**
  - **Substantive Review (1.5 hrs):** Wills & Estates - Components of a Will (Integration, Codicils, Incorporation by Reference), Basic Trust Introduction (Creation requirements, Types - intro).
  - **Timed Mixed MBE Set (1.5 hrs):** 40-50 MBE questions, **timed**. Mix of all 7 MBE subjects.
  - **Brief Review (30 mins):** Score MBE set. Quick review of 5-10 incorrects.
- **Afternoon Block - MPT Focus:**
  - **MPT Timed Practice (1.5 hrs):** Take one full MPT under strict timed conditions (90 minutes). Use the 45/45 strategy (or your adjusted version). **Practice finishing on time.**
  - **MPT Self-Critique (1.5 hrs):** Immediately after, do a thorough comparison to the model answer and point sheet. Did your timing strategy work? Were you able to outline effectively in the first half? Did you translate the outline into a coherent written product in the second half? Where did you fall short? Be specific and honest.
- **Evening Block:**

- **Review (1.5 hrs):** Thorough review of incorrect MBEs from the morning set. Consolidate Wills & Estates notes, including basic Trust concepts.

Day 5: Friday

- **Morning Block:**
  - **Targeted Substantive Review (1.5 hrs):** Pick 1-2 MBE or MEE subjects where you feel weakest based on recent practice. Do a focused review of key rules/concepts.
  - **Timed Mixed MBE Set (1.5 hrs):** 40-50 MBE questions, **timed**. Mix of all 7 MBE subjects.
  - **Brief Review (30 mins):** Score MBE set. Quick review of 5-10 incorrects.
- **Afternoon Block - Timed Essay Barrage:**
  - **Timed Essay 1 (30 mins):** Pick an essay prompt (e.g., Contracts or Torts). Write full answer timed.
  - **Brief Break (5-10 mins):** Stand up, stretch.
  - **Timed Essay 2 (30 mins):** Pick another essay prompt (e.g., Evidence or Civ Pro). Write full answer timed.
  - **Brief Break (5-10 mins):**
  - **Timed Essay 3 (Optional but Recommended) (30 mins):** Pick a third prompt (e.g., Family Law or Wills). Write full answer timed.
  - **Essay Self-Critique (1 hr):** Review all essays written today against model answers. Focus on speed, issue spotting, concise IRAC under pressure. Identify patterns in what you miss when rushed.
- **Evening Block:**
  - **Review (1.5 hrs):** Thorough review of incorrect MBEs from the morning. Deeper review of insights gained from the timed essay practice.

Day 6: Saturday

- **Morning Block (e.g., 9:00 AM - 1:00 PM):**

- **Timed Mixed MBE Practice (3 hrs):** 100 MBE questions, timed (3 hours). Mix covering all 7 MBE subjects. Continued endurance building.
- **Review (1 hr):** Score the MBE set. Calculate overall % and % by subject. Note initial thoughts. Take a break.

- **Afternoon Block (e.g., 2:00 PM - 5:00 PM):**
  - **MBE Explanation Review (3 hrs):** Deep dive into the explanations for the 100-question set. Continue identifying persistent weak areas or types of errors (rule gaps, reading comp, time pressure mistakes).
- **Evening: REST.** Mandatory.

Day 7: Sunday

- **Option 1 (Targeted Timed Practice):** Use 2-3 hours to do more timed practice focused on your weakest areas. E.g., 30 timed MBE questions on that subject, or writing 1-2 more timed essays on specific topics.
- **Option 2 (Review & Planning):** Use 1-2 hours to review notes, especially for Family Law & Wills/Estates, and plan logistics for Week 6 (Simulation!).
- **Afternoon/Evening: REST and Recharge.** Prepare mentally for the first full simulated exam experience next week.

Weekend Structure Summary

Week 5's weekend continues the established pattern: a long timed MBE set on Saturday morning followed by extensive review. The key difference is the *context* – you're now reviewing performance after a week focused heavily on increasing speed across all components. Sunday provides a crucial opportunity for targeted reinforcement or essential rest before heading into simulation territory.

Picking Up the Pace Sensibly

Week 5 demanded more – more subjects, more speed, more pressure. You practiced writing faster, thinking faster, managing time more aggressively. It likely felt chaotic at times, maybe even frantic. That's the nature of ramping up practice. The rational perspective is that you *subjected* yourself to that pressure deliberately. You didn't demand instant, perfect speed; you *practiced* the actions that build speed. You gathered more data on how you perform under timed conditions. Accept that data without unnecessary self-flagellation ("I *should* be faster by now!"). You are exactly where you are. The consistent application of timed practice, coupled with review, is the only sensible way forward. Now, get ready to put it all together in a simulated exam environment in Week 6.

Key Takeaways for Week 5

- Introduced and covered core concepts of Family Law and Wills & Estates.
- Significantly increased the frequency and emphasis on **timed practice** for MBE sets, full essays (aiming for 30 mins), and MPTs (aiming for 90 mins).
- Focused on building speed and efficiency alongside knowledge recall.
- Practiced managing the feeling of being spread thin across many subjects while pushing for speed.
- Challenged perfectionistic demands about performance under timed conditions, focusing instead on the process of persistent practice and gradual improvement.
- Continued the routine of substantial weekend MBE practice and review, along with essential rest.

Okay, we're entering the final stretch – the last three weeks. You've covered the bulk of the substantive law, you've practiced different formats, and you've started integrating subjects and working under timed conditions. These last weeks are about putting it all together, refining your approach, and getting mentally prepared for the actual exam days. Week 6 features the crucial first full simulated exam – a dress rehearsal that provides invaluable feedback. Week 7 is about peak practice, hitting your weak areas hard based on that feedback. And Week 8 focuses on final polishing, logistics, and managing the inevitable pre-exam jitters. Don't ease up yet, but also don't fall prey to frantic, unproductive panic. Stick to the plan, trust the process you've followed, and keep challenging those unhelpful thoughts that are bound to pop up.

Chapter 10: Week 6 - Simulation and Refinement

This is a big week. We'll briefly cover the final MEE subjects often tested (like Trusts and Secured Transactions, though check your jurisdiction!), but the main event is your **first full simulated bar exam**. This means sitting for two days under realistic timed conditions, mimicking the MPT/MEE day and the MBE day. The prospect might fill you with dread ("What if I fail miserably?! It will prove I'm hopeless!"). Utter nonsense. The purpose of this simulation is **not** to perfectly predict your score or to serve as a final judgment. It's a **diagnostic tool** on steroids and invaluable **practice for the *process***. It reveals weaknesses in knowledge, timing, and endurance under full exam pressure. The score itself is secondary to the feedback you gain. Approach it as an information-gathering exercise and a chance to practice managing your energy and focus over two demanding days. Accepting whatever happens without awfulizing is key to learning from it.

Weekly Overview

- **Goals for the Week:**
    - Cover core concepts of Trusts and Secured Transactions (UCC Art. 9 basics). Briefly review Conflict of Laws principles (often integrated into other essays).
    - Complete the **first full 2-day simulated bar exam** under strict timed conditions.
    - Begin refining strategies based on simulated exam performance.
    - Continue daily review of incorrect answers and model answers, especially focusing on simulation feedback.
- **Subjects Covered:**
    - MEE: Trusts, Secured Transactions, Conflict of Laws (integrated review).
    - Review: All MBE subjects and previously covered MEE subjects.
    - Skills: Full 2-day simulated exam practice, analyzing simulation results, targeted refinement.
- **Key Tasks:**

- Substantive review of Trusts & Secured Transactions early in the week (approx. 1.5-2 hours/day Mon-Tues).
- Complete full simulated exam (e.g., Thurs/Fri). Day 1: MPT session (e.g., 2 MPTs, 3 hrs) + MEE session (e.g., 6 Essays, 3 hrs). Day 2: MBE session 1 (e.g., 100 Qs, 3 hrs) + MBE session 2 (e.g., 100 Qs, 3 hrs). **Use actual released questions if possible.**
- Dedicate significant time over the weekend to **thoroughly review** the entire simulated exam.
- Light MBE/essay practice early week; focus shifts to simulation mid-week.

- **Mindset Focus for the Week: Simulation as Feedback, Not Foreboding**
  - The simulation score might not be what you hope for. You might feel exhausted or discouraged afterward. The irrational thought is: "This horrible score *proves* I'll fail the real exam!"
  - **Challenge:** A simulation score is just one data point from one specific set of questions on one particular day. It doesn't magically predict the future. Its value lies in the **process feedback** (How was your timing? Where did your energy flag? Did your strategies work?) and the **content feedback** (What specific rules did you miss? What types of analysis were weak?).
  - **Rational Alternative:** "I accept whatever score I get on this simulation without demanding it *must* be higher. The score is just information. I will focus on the *process* of taking the full exam and analyze the results objectively to identify specific areas for improvement in Weeks 7 and 8. This simulation is a tool for learning and refinement, not a crystal ball foretelling doom."

Daily Schedule Day 1 - Day 7

(Schedule accommodates full simulation Thurs/Fri)

Day 1: Monday

- **Morning Block:**

- **Substantive Review (1.5 hrs):** Trusts - Creation (Intent, Trustee, Beneficiary, Property, Purpose), Types (Express, Resulting, Constructive - basics).
- **Timed Mixed MBE Set (1.5 hrs):** 40-50 MBE questions, **timed**. Mix of all 7 MBE subjects. Reinforce speed/accuracy.
- **Brief Review (30 mins):** Score MBE set. Quick review of 5-10 incorrects.

- **Afternoon Block:**
  - **Substantive Review (1.5 hrs):** Trusts - Trustee Duties (Loyalty, Care, Prudence), Modification/Termination of Trusts.
  - **Essay Practice (1 hr):** Find a Trusts essay. **Outline** timed (10-15 mins). Write full essay **untimed** (focus on clarity of rules/application).
  - **(Optional MBE: 30 mins - 15-20 Qs targeted on a known weak area).**
- **Evening Block:**
  - **Review (1.5 hrs):** Thorough review of incorrect MBEs. Compare Trusts essay to model. Start Trusts notes.

Day 2: Tuesday

- **Morning Block:**
  - **Substantive Review (1.5 hrs):** Secured Transactions (UCC Art. 9) - Scope, Attachment (Security Agreement, Value, Rights).
  - **Timed Mixed MBE Set (1.5 hrs):** 40-50 MBE questions, **timed**. Mix of all 7 MBE subjects.
  - **Brief Review (30 mins):** Score MBE set. Quick review of 5-10 incorrects.
- **Afternoon Block:**
  - **Substantive Review (1.5 hrs):** Secured Transactions - Perfection (Filing, Possession, Control, Automatic), Priority Rules (Basics: Perfected vs. Unperfected, Perfected vs. Perfected, PMSIs).

- **Essay Practice (1 hr):** Find a Secured Transactions essay (if available, focus on attachment/perfection). **Outline** timed (10-15 mins). Write full essay **untimed**.
- **(Optional MEE Review: 30 mins - Review Conflict of Laws basic approaches - integrated into other subjects).**

- **Evening Block:**
  - **Review (1.5 hrs):** Thorough review of incorrect MBEs. Compare Secured Trans essay to model. Start Secured Transactions notes.

Day 3: Wednesday - Simulation Prep & Light Review

- **Morning Block:**
  - **Light Review (1.5 hrs):** Quickly review attack outlines or flashcards for your 2-3 weakest subjects overall (identified from Week 4 check-in or recent practice). Do NOT try to cram new material.
  - **Timed Mixed MBE Set (1 hr):** 25-30 MBE questions, timed. Just keeping the engine warm.
  - **Review MBEs (30 mins):** Quick review of incorrects.
- **Afternoon Block:**
  - **Simulation Logistics (1 hr):** Prepare everything for the next two days. Confirm materials (practice exam booklets/software, scratch paper, pens, timer, water, snacks). Plan your schedule for Thursday/Friday including start times, break times, lunch. Mimic actual exam day logistics as much as possible. Charge your laptop!
  - **Mental Prep / Relaxation (2+ hrs):** Read Chapter 16 on Exam Day Strategy. Practice stress management techniques (deep breathing, visualization). Do something relaxing – take a walk, listen to music. **Avoid heavy studying.** Your brain needs to be fresh for tomorrow.
- **Evening: REST.** Eat a good meal. Get to bed early. Treat tonight like the night before Day 1 of the real exam.

Day 4: Thursday - Simulated Exam Day 1 (MPT & MEE)

- **Follow Exam Day Schedule:** Start at the time your actual exam begins.
- **Morning Session (e.g., 3 hours):** Complete 2 MPTs under strict timed conditions (90 mins each).[1] Use your practiced timing strategy (e.g., 45/45).
- **Lunch Break (e.g., 1 hour):** Mimic exam day break. Get away from study materials. Eat something sensible.
- **Afternoon Session (e.g., 3 hours):** Complete 6 MEEs (or your jurisdiction's equivalent) under strict timed conditions (30 mins each). Move on after 30 minutes, even if unfinished!
- **Evening: STOP.** Put materials away. Do **not** start grading or reviewing yet. Your brain is fried. Relax, eat dinner, do something completely unrelated to law. Recover.

Day 5: Friday - Simulated Exam Day 2 (MBE)

- **Follow Exam Day Schedule:** Start at the same time as yesterday.
- **Morning Session (e.g., 3 hours):** Complete 100 MBE questions under strict timed conditions.
- **Lunch Break (e.g., 1 hour):** Same as yesterday – real break.
- **Afternoon Session (e.g., 3 hours):** Complete another 100 MBE questions under strict timed conditions.
- **Evening: STOP.** You did it! You completed a full simulated bar exam. Acknowledge the effort. **Do not start grading tonight.** Put everything away. Relax, have a good meal, maybe watch a mindless movie. Let your brain defragment overnight.

Day 6: Saturday - Simulation Review Part 1 (MBE & MPT)

- **Morning Block (e.g., 9:00 AM - 1:00 PM):**
    - **MBE Scoring & Review (4 hrs):** Score both 100-question MBE sections. Calculate overall % and % by subject. Now, begin the **deep review** of explanations, focusing on incorrect answers. Aim to get through explanations for the first 100 questions (or as many as feasible with

quality review). Note specific rules missed and error types (rule gap, reading error, time pressure, etc.).

- **Afternoon Block (e.g., 2:00 PM - 5:00 PM):**
  - **MPT Review (3 hrs):** Using model answers and point sheets, carefully review both MPTs you completed on Thursday. How did your timing work in practice? Did you follow the task memo? Spot key issues/facts/rules? Structure it logically? Where did you lose points? Be brutally honest.

Day 7: Sunday - Simulation Review Part 2 (MEE & Synthesis)

- **Morning Block (e.g., 9:00 AM - 1:00 PM):**
  - **MEE Review (4 hrs):** Using model answers/grading guides, carefully review all 6 MEEs from Thursday. Assess issue spotting, rule statements, analysis (applying facts!), and organization for each. Where were the major point losses? Which subjects felt weakest under pressure?
- **Afternoon Block (e.g., 2:00 PM - 4:00 PM):**
  - **Synthesize & Plan (2 hrs):** Look at your performance across *all* sections (MBE subjects, MEE subjects, MPT skills). Synthesize the data. What are the 3-5 **most critical weak areas** you need to attack in Week 7? Be specific (e.g., "MBE Hearsay Exceptions," "Applying facts in Contracts essays," "MPT Persuasive Brief timing," "Rule Against Perpetuities - still!"). Write down your attack plan for Week 7.
- **Evening: REST and Recharge.** The review process is exhausting too. Prepare for an intense Week 7 focused on targeted practice.

Weekend Structure Summary

Week 6 weekend is **entirely dedicated to reviewing the simulated exam**. This review is arguably more important than the simulation itself. It requires significant time and honest self-assessment across all components. The goal is not just to see the score, but to **extract actionable intelligence** to guide your final phase of study. Sunday afternoon's synthesis and planning step is crucial for translating the review into a targeted attack plan for Week 7.

Surviving the Dress Rehearsal

Completing a full simulated bar exam is a major accomplishment, regardless of how you feel about your performance. You subjected yourself to the grueling pace and mental demands of the real thing. The review process this weekend was likely intense, perhaps revealing areas that need serious work. Excellent. That's precisely the point. You now have highly specific, personalized data about where to focus your remaining energy. Don't indulge in catastrophizing about low scores or demanding that you *should* have done better. Accept the results as valuable feedback. Use the insights gained to sharpen your focus and attack your weaknesses with targeted practice in Week 7. You survived the dress rehearsal; now use what you learned to prepare for opening night.

Key Takeaways for Week 6

- Covered final MEE subjects like Trusts and Secured Transactions.
- Successfully completed a full 2-day simulated bar exam under realistic timed conditions.
- Practiced managing time, energy, and focus over the full duration of the exam.
- Understood the simulation's primary value as a diagnostic tool and feedback mechanism, not a definitive prediction.
- Dedicated the entire weekend to a thorough, multi-part review of MBE, MEE, and MPT performance from the simulation.
- Synthesized simulation feedback to identify the most critical weak areas requiring targeted attack in Week 7.
- Challenged perfectionistic demands about simulation scores, focusing instead on learning from the process and results.

Chapter 11: Week 7 - Peak Practice & Weak Area Attack

This is it – the penultimate week. Week 6's simulation gave you invaluable data on your strengths and, more importantly, your weaknesses under pressure. Week 7 is about leveraging that information. The focus shifts decisively towards **peak practice intensity** and a **targeted attack on those specific weak areas** you identified. Expect lots of timed, mixed practice across all formats (MBE, MEE, MPT), simulating exam conditions as closely as possible in your daily work. There's no new substantive law; the goal now is refinement, reinforcement, and shoring up the areas where you need the most points. You might feel fatigue setting in, or perhaps a sense of plateau where scores aren't jumping dramatically despite hard work. It's tempting to think, "This isn't working! I *must* be seeing huge gains by now!" Challenge that. Improvement isn't always linear, especially at this stage. Trust the cumulative effect of consistent, targeted practice. Focus on executing your weak area attack plan and maintaining disciplined effort.

Weekly Overview

- **Goals for the Week:**
  - Execute targeted attack plan on 3-5 weakest areas identified from Week 6 simulation review.
  - Engage in heavy, timed, mixed practice across MBE, MEE, and MPT formats daily.
  - Maintain simulated exam conditions (timing, limited distractions) during practice blocks.[2]
  - Refine exam-taking strategies (e.g., time management per question/essay, approach for difficult questions).[3]
  - Manage fatigue and maintain focus through consistent routines and scheduled breaks.
- **Subjects Covered:**
  - **All subjects** integrated into mixed practice. Targeted review focused on identified weak areas.

- **Skills:** High-frequency timed mixed MBE sets, multiple timed essays daily or every other day, regular timed MPT practice, strategy refinement.
- **Key Tasks:**
    - Daily timed mixed MBE sets (e.g., 50-100 questions).
    - Daily timed essay practice (e.g., 2-3 essays covering mixed subjects, including weak areas).
    - Complete 1-2 timed MPTs, focusing on strategy execution.
    - Dedicate specific review blocks *daily* to rules/concepts within identified weak areas.
    - Consistent review of all practice problems, focusing on *why* errors occurred (rule gap? misreading? time pressure?).
- **Mindset Focus for the Week: Trusting the Process, Managing Plateau Panic**
    - As intensity peaks, results might level off temporarily. This "plateau" can trigger panic: "I'm stuck! All this work is for nothing! I *should* be improving faster!"
    - **Challenge:** Improvement often happens in steps, not smooth curves. Scores might fluctuate. Focusing only on scores ignores progress in speed, issue spotting consistency, or rule recall accuracy. Demanding constant, visible improvement is irrational.
    - **Rational Alternative:** "I accept that progress might not always be obvious day-to-day. My focus is on consistently executing my study plan, especially attacking my weak areas with deliberate practice. I trust that this sustained, targeted effort is building the necessary skills and knowledge, even if my scores plateau temporarily. I will measure progress by my adherence to the plan and my understanding during review, not just daily scores."

Daily Schedule Day 1 - Day 7

(Schedule emphasizes integrated practice and weak area focus)

Day 1: Monday

- **Morning Block (e.g., 8:30 AM - 12:30 PM):**
  - **Timed Mixed MBE Set (2 hrs):** 60-70 MBE questions, timed (~1.8 min/q). Mix of all 7 subjects.
  - **MBE Review (2 hrs):** Thorough review of explanations, focusing on incorrect answers. Note any errors related to identified weak areas.
- **Afternoon Block (e.g., 1:30 PM - 5:00 PM):**
  - **Timed Essay Practice (1.5 hrs):** Write 3 essays back-to-back, **timed** (30 mins each). Choose subjects that include 1-2 of your identified weak areas.
  - **Essay Review (1.5 hrs):** Review all 3 essays against model answers. Focus on accuracy and analysis, especially in weak area subjects. Did you apply the correct rules under pressure?
  - **Weak Area Review (1 hr):** Targeted review of notes or outlines specifically for one of your top weak areas (e.g., Hearsay exceptions, PJ analysis steps, Negligence defenses).
- **Evening Block (e.g., 6:00 PM - 7:30 PM):**
  - **Consolidated Review / Light Planning (1.5 hrs):** Review key takeaways/errors from the day across all practice. Briefly plan Tuesday's weak area focus.

Day 2: Tuesday

- **Morning Block (e.g., 8:30 AM - 12:30 PM):**
  - **Timed Mixed MBE Set (2.5 hrs):** 80-90 MBE questions, timed. Mix of all 7 subjects. Build endurance.
  - **MBE Review (1.5 hrs):** Thorough review of explanations, focusing on incorrects. Note errors in weak areas.
- **Afternoon Block (e.g., 1:30 PM - 5:00 PM):**
  - **Timed MPT Practice (1.5 hrs):** Complete 1 full MPT under timed conditions (90 mins). Focus on executing your timing strategy efficiently.

    - **MPT Review (1.5 hrs):** Thoroughly review MPT against model answer/point sheet. Assess timing, structure, analysis. Was it an improvement over last week's?
    - **Weak Area Review (1 hr):** Targeted review specifically for a second identified weak area (e.g., Contract formation issues, Character evidence rules, SMJ concepts).
- **Evening Block (e.g., 6:00 PM - 7:30 PM):**
    - **Consolidated Review / Light Planning (1.5 hrs):** Review key takeaways/errors from the day. Briefly plan Wednesday's weak area focus.

Day 3: Wednesday

- **Morning Block (e.g., 8:30 AM - 12:30 PM):**
    - **Timed Mixed MBE Set (3 hrs):** 100 MBE questions, timed. Full morning simulation.
    - **MBE Review (1 hr):** Score the set. Do a quick review of explanations for ~20 particularly troublesome incorrect answers. Deeper review tonight.
- **Afternoon Block (e.g., 1:30 PM - 5:00 PM):**
    - **Timed Essay Practice (1.5 hrs):** Write 3 essays back-to-back, **timed** (30 mins each). Mix subjects, ensuring coverage of weak areas.
    - **Essay Review (1.5 hrs):** Review all 3 essays against models. Focus on speed and hitting key analytical points.
    - **Weak Area Review (1 hr):** Targeted review for a third identified weak area (e.g., Real Property future interests, Con Law levels of scrutiny, Corp D&O duties).
- **Evening Block (e.g., 6:00 PM - 7:30 PM):**
    - **MBE Deep Review (1.5 hrs):** Continue thorough review of explanations from the morning's 100-question MBE set.

Day 4: Thursday

- **Morning Block (e.g., 8:30 AM - 12:30 PM):**
    - **Timed Mixed MBE Set (2 hrs):** 60-70 MBE questions, timed.
    - **MBE Review (2 hrs):** Thorough review of explanations.
- **Afternoon Block (e.g., 1:30 PM - 5:00 PM):**
    - **Optional Timed MPT (1.5 hrs):** If MPT is a significant weakness, do another timed MPT + 1 hr review.
    - **OR Timed Essay Practice (1.5 hrs):** Write 3 timed essays + 1 hr review.
    - **Weak Area Review Block (1 hr):** Choose the weak area needing most attention based on recent practice. Do targeted drills, review flashcards, re-read outline sections.
- **Evening Block (e.g., 6:00 PM - 7:30 PM):**
    - **Consolidated Review / Strategy Refinement (1.5 hrs):** Review errors. Think about test-taking strategy: Are you managing time well per MBE question? How do you approach essays you feel shaky on? Are you outlining MPTs effectively?

Day 5: Friday

- **Morning Block (e.g., 8:30 AM - 12:30 PM):**
    - **Timed Mixed MBE Set (2.5 hrs):** 80-90 MBE questions, timed.
    - **MBE Review (1.5 hrs):** Thorough review of explanations.
- **Afternoon Block (e.g., 1:30 PM - 5:00 PM):**
    - **Timed Essay Practice (1.5 hrs):** Write 3 essays back-to-back, timed (30 mins each). Mix subjects.
    - **Essay Review (1.5 hrs):** Review essays against models.
    - **Weak Area Review (1 hr):** Final targeted review session for the week on a key weak area.
- **Evening Block (e.g., 6:00 PM - 7:00 PM):**

    - **Light Review / Prep for Weekend (1 hr):** Look over notes briefly. Tidy up study area. Mentally prepare for weekend practice. **Stop studying early tonight.**

Day 6: Saturday

- **Morning Block (e.g., 9:00 AM - 1:00 PM):**
    - **Practice Simulation (Approx. 3-4 hrs):** Choose one, simulating exam conditions:
        - Option A: 100 Timed Mixed MBE questions (3 hours).
        - Option B: MPT Session (2 Timed MPTs, 3 hours).
        - Option C: MEE Session (6 Timed Essays, 3 hours).
    - **Scoring/Initial Impressions (30 mins):** Score work. Note thoughts. Break.
- **Afternoon Block (e.g., 2:00 PM - 5:00 PM):**
    - **Practice Review (3 hrs):** Thorough review of explanations/model answers for the morning's simulation block. Focus on strategy execution and persistent errors, especially in weak areas.
- **Evening: REST.** Crucial recovery time.

Day 7: Sunday

- **Review & Synthesis (2-3 hours):** Review notes from the week, particularly focusing on weak area work and insights from practice simulations. Did the targeted attack seem effective? What needs focus in the final week? Synthesize key rules or attack plans.
- **Afternoon/Evening: REST and Recharge.** Prepare mentally for the final week. Do something enjoyable and relaxing.

Weekend Structure Summary

Week 7's weekend continues the pattern of significant timed practice under simulated conditions on Saturday, followed by deep review. The choice of simulation block (MBE, MPT, or MEE) might be guided by which area felt weakest or needs the most strategy refinement. Sunday is for consolidating the week's learning, synthesizing key takeaways, and crucial mental and physical rest before the final push in Week 8.

The Final Push Strategy Over Strain

Week 7 was about intense, focused effort directed at your specific needs. You bombarded your weaknesses, pushed through heavy mixed practice, and kept simulating exam conditions. If you felt tired or like you hit a wall, that's understandable – peak exertion takes its toll. The key now is not to panic or resort to frantic, unstructured cramming. It's about trusting the cumulative work you've done. You know more than you think you do. The final week isn't primarily about learning new things; it's about consolidating what you know, polishing your approach, managing your mindset, and ensuring you arrive at the exam hall as prepared and calm as possible. Strategy over strain is the motto now.

Key Takeaways for Week 7

- Executed a targeted attack plan on weak areas identified from the Week 6 simulation.
- Engaged in high-volume, timed, mixed practice across MBE, MEE, and MPT formats to simulate exam conditions and build endurance.
- Focused on refining exam-taking strategies for timing, question approach, and managing pressure.
- Practiced managing fatigue and potential feelings of plateauing by trusting the process and focusing on consistent, targeted effort.
- Challenged irrational beliefs about linear improvement, emphasizing the cumulative effect of sustained practice.
- Continued weekend simulation practice and review, alongside essential rest.

Chapter 12: Week 8 - Final Polish and Exam Readiness

This is the final week before the exam. The hay is mostly in the barn. The goal now is **not** to cram frantically or learn vast amounts of new material – that's likely counterproductive and anxiety-inducing. Instead, Week 8 focuses on **final polishing, logistical preparation, and intensive mindset management**. Think light review of key concepts, memorizing critical checklists or attack outlines, confirming all exam day logistics, and actively managing stress and pre-exam anxiety.[4] You might feel a strong urge to study constantly, driven by the irrational fear that "If I stop, I'll forget everything!" or the demand "I *must* use every last second productively!" Resist this. Tapering down the intensity, building confidence, and ensuring you are well-rested are far more beneficial now than exhausting yourself with last-minute cramming.

Weekly Overview

- **Goals for the Week:**
  - Light review of high-frequency rules, personal weak areas, and attack outlines/checklists.
  - Active memorization of key elements/frameworks.
  - Finalize all exam day logistics (travel, packing, site rules).
  - Implement intensive stress management and positive mindset strategies.
  - Gradually taper down study intensity to ensure adequate rest before Day 1.
  - (Optional) Complete one final short practice simulation early in the week if desired.
- **Subjects Covered:**
  - Light, targeted review across all subjects based on personal notes, attack outlines, and identified persistent weaknesses. No deep dives into new or complex areas.
- **Skills:** Memorization techniques, logistical planning, stress reduction, mindset reinforcement. Limited, optional timed practice early in the week.

- **Key Tasks:**
  - Daily light review using flashcards, attack outlines, checklists (focus on recall).
  - Confirm all exam logistics: location, timing, rules, what to bring/not bring.[5]
  - Practice relaxation/stress management techniques daily.
  - Positive self-talk and challenging catastrophic thinking *constantly*.
  - Prioritize sleep, healthy eating, and light exercise/relaxation.
  - **Significantly reduce study hours** by mid-week; very light review day before exam; **no studying night before.**
- **Mindset Focus for the Week: Radical Acceptance and Focusing on Controllables**
  - Pre-exam anxiety is almost guaranteed. You might catastrophize: "What if I get sick? What if I blank out? What if the MPT is bizarre? What if I fail and waste all this effort?!" These "what ifs" spiral easily.
  - **Challenge:** Trying to eliminate anxiety entirely is impossible and fighting it makes it worse. Demanding certainty about the exam or the outcome is irrational.
  - **Rational Alternative:** "**Radically accept** the uncertainty and the anxiety. Acknowledge the feelings without letting them dictate your actions or beliefs ('Okay, I feel anxious, that's normal before a big event'). **Focus intensely on what you *can* control**: your preparation routines this week (light review, logistics, self-care), your adherence to your strategies *during* the exam (timing, approach), and actively challenging your own negative self-talk. You cannot control the specific questions asked or the final outcome, but you *can* control your preparation and your responses. Trust the work you've done over the past seven weeks."

Daily Schedule Day 1 - Day 7 (Exam Week!)

(Tapering Schedule: Reduce hours & intensity as week progresses)

Day 1: Monday (Approx. 6-7 hours study)

- **Morning Block (e.g., 9:00 AM - 12:00 PM):**
  - **Light Review & Memorization (1.5 hrs):** Review attack outlines/flashcards for 2-3 subjects (e.g., your weakest MBE subjects, or key MEE frameworks like Bus Ass duties). Focus on active recall.
  - **Optional Timed Practice (1.5 hrs):** Choose ONE short session IF you feel it builds confidence (do NOT do this if it increases anxiety):
    - 30-40 Timed Mixed MBE Questions + Quick Review.
    - 1-2 Timed Essays on weak/key subjects + Quick Review.
    - Outline 1 MPT + Quick Review vs Model Outline.
  - **If NO practice:** Extend light review/memorization to 3 hrs.
- **Afternoon Block (e.g., 1:00 PM - 4:00 PM):**
  - **Light Review & Memorization (2 hrs):** Review attack outlines/flashcards for 2-3 different subjects. Use different methods (recite aloud, rewrite from memory).
  - **Logistics Check (1 hr):** Review exam site rules (what's allowed/prohibited). Plan your exam day outfits (comfort!). Start packing your exam bag (ID, admission ticket, permitted supplies, water, snacks, meds). Double-check travel plans/timing.
- **Evening: STOP Studying.** Relax. Light exercise. Healthy dinner. Good sleep.

Day 2: Tuesday (Approx. 5-6 hours study)

- **Morning Block (e.g., 9:00 AM - 12:00 PM):**
  - **Light Review & Memorization (3 hrs):** Focus on high-frequency MEE subjects or remaining MBE subjects using outlines/flashcards. Drill key elements, tests, exceptions. Keep it active, not passive reading.
- **Afternoon Block (e.g., 1:00 PM - 3:30 PM):**

- **Light Review & Memorization (1.5 hrs):** Final pass through your most critical checklists or "panic points." Maybe review MPT formats/timing strategy one last time.
- **Stress Management Practice (1 hr):** Practice deep breathing, visualization (seeing yourself calm and focused during the exam), or mindfulness. Read positive affirmations or reinforcing statements about the effort you've put in. Challenge any negative thoughts that arise.

- **Evening: STOP Studying.** Pack your lunch/snacks for Day 1 if allowed. Lay out clothes. Relax completely. Watch something funny. Avoid stressful conversations. **Prioritize sleep.**

Day 3: Wednesday (Day Before Exam - Approx. 0-2 hours LIGHT activity)

- **Morning: NO heavy studying.** Maybe a 30-60 minute MAX very light flick-through of flashcards or attack outlines *only if it genuinely calms your nerves*. If it makes you anxious, DON'T DO IT.
- **Logistics:** Drive to the exam center if unfamiliar to check route/parking. Confirm travel times. Final check of exam bag.
- **Activity:** Focus on **relaxation and calm**. Light exercise like a walk. Listen to music. Watch a movie. Meditate. Eat healthy meals. Stay hydrated.
- **Mindset: Actively challenge catastrophic thoughts.** Use positive self-talk. Remind yourself you've prepared thoroughly using a structured plan. Trust your preparation. Accept the anxiety, don't fight it. Visualize success (navigating the exam calmly and competently).
- **Evening: Absolutely NO studying or cramming.** Have a calm dinner. Final logistics check. Set multiple alarms. Go to bed early, even if you don't feel tired. Read something light and unrelated to law if needed.

Day 4: Thursday - EXAM DAY 1 (MPT/MEE)

- **Morning:** Wake up with alarms. Eat a good breakfast (protein, complex carbs – avoid sugar crash). Hydrate. Do a brief relaxation exercise (e.g., 5 mins deep breathing). Arrive at the test center with plenty of time, but not *so* early you sit around getting anxious. Avoid panicked chatter with other test-takers. Focus inward.

- **During Exam Sessions:**
  - **Execute Your Strategies:** Remember your timing for MPTs (e.g., 45/45) and essays (30 mins). Stick to it.
  - **Manage Anxiety:** If you feel panic rising, take 15-30 seconds for deep breaths. Remind yourself you can handle it.
  - **Difficult Questions:** If you hit a tough essay or confusing MPT, make your best educated guess or structured analysis and *move on*. Don't get bogged down. One question won't determine your fate.
  - **Focus:** Stay focused on the current question/task only. Don't worry about past sections or future ones.
- **Lunch Break:** Get away from the exam room. Eat your packed lunch. Don't discuss morning questions with others (it's pointless and often anxiety-provoking). Stretch, get fresh air if possible. Reset mentally.
- **Afternoon Session:** Re-engage with focus. Execute your timing strategy.
- **Evening: DONE with Day 1!** Do **NOT** debrief or analyze your performance. It's over. Do **NOT** study for Day 2. Eat a good dinner. Relax as much as possible (movie, music, talk to supportive person about non-exam things). Prepare logistically for Day 2. Get sleep.

Day 5: Friday - EXAM DAY 2 (MBE)

- **Morning:** Same routine as yesterday – good breakfast, hydration, relaxation, arrive with adequate time. Avoid anxious crowds.
- **During Exam Sessions:**
  - **Pacing:** Keep track of your timing per question (~1.8 mins). If you fall behind, make a note to catch up slightly on easier questions later. Don't rush wildly.

- **Difficult Questions:** If stuck, eliminate clearly wrong answers, make your best guess among the remainder, flag it (if allowed/useful), and *move on*. Don't spend 5 minutes on one question.
- **Endurance:** MBE day is long. Use the break between sessions effectively. Stay hydrated and maintain blood sugar with sensible snacks if allowed.

- **Lunch Break:** Same as yesterday – escape, refuel, reset. Don't talk questions.
- **Afternoon Session:** Final push. Maintain focus and pacing. Trust your preparation.
- **End of Exam: YOU FINISHED!** Celebrate this monumental achievement. Acknowledge the incredible effort regardless of how you *feel* you performed.

Day 6 & 7 (Post-Exam Weekend):

- **REST. RECOVER. DETACH.** Do absolutely nothing related to the bar exam. Don't look up answers. Don't read forums dissecting questions (it's torture!). Reconnect with life, friends, family, hobbies. Sleep. Eat well. Allow your brain and body to recover from the marathon. Congratulate yourself for surviving the process.

Weekend Structure Summary

The "weekend" structure for Week 8 is dominated by the exam itself and the immediate recovery period. The focus shifts entirely from structured study to executing exam strategies, managing mindset in real-time, and then completely detaching post-exam for essential recovery.

Walking In Prepared and Reasonably Calm

You made it through the 8-week gauntlet and the two days of the exam itself. The final week wasn't about frantic last-minute learning; it was about consolidating, preparing logistically, and most importantly, managing your own mind. You faced the anxiety, hopefully challenged the catastrophic thoughts, and focused on what you could control. Walking into that exam hall, the goal wasn't to be magically free of nerves – that's unrealistic. The goal was to be *prepared*, *logistically ready*, and *reasonably calm*, equipped with strategies to handle the pressure and trust the enormous amount of work you put in. Regardless of the eventual outcome (which you cannot control now), completing this rigorous preparation process and sitting for the exam is a testament to your discipline and resilience. Now, truly let it go and allow yourself to recover.

Key Takeaways for Week 8

- Shifted focus from heavy practice to light review, memorization of key frameworks/rules, and logistical preparation.
- Prioritized stress management, mindset reinforcement, and actively challenging catastrophic pre-exam thoughts.
- Tapered study intensity significantly mid-week, with minimal activity the day before the exam to ensure rest.
- Executed pre-planned exam day routines for arrival, breaks, and managing anxiety/difficult questions during the test.
- Understood the importance of **not** studying the night before or between exam days, and **not** debriefing performance immediately after.
- Focused on radical acceptance of uncertainty and anxiety, concentrating effort on controllable factors like preparation and strategy execution.
- Recognized the necessity of complete detachment and rest in the days immediately following the exam.

Part 3: Strategy, Execution, and Beyond

Okay, the 8-week schedule laid out in Part 2 provided the structure and the 'what-to-do' on a daily basis. Now, in Part 3, we shift focus slightly. We'll look at refining your techniques for each part of the exam, understanding how to truly learn from your practice, and navigating the final crucial period – the last week and the exam days themselves. Knowing the law is necessary, sure, but it's often not sufficient. Passing requires strategy, effective analysis of your own performance, and perhaps most importantly, managing your own head throughout the process. Let's get into the practicalities of maximizing your performance beyond just hitting the books according to schedule.

Chapter 13: Mastering the Components - Advanced Techniques

You've spent weeks practicing the MBE, essays, and MPTs according to the schedule. You know the basic formats. Now, let's talk about adding some finesse—some specific techniques to handle each component more effectively and efficiently. Don't mistake these for magic tricks; they are **rational tools** built on understanding how the test works and how to manage your time and thinking under pressure. Thinking you *must* already know all this, or that applying these techniques *should* feel easy immediately, is just setting yourself up for frustration. These are skills, and like any skill, they improve with deliberate practice.

MBE Strategy Timing Elimination techniques common traps

The MBE is a beast of speed and precision. With only about 1.8 minutes per question, you need more than just legal knowledge. You need a system.

1. **Timing is Everything (Almost):** You *must* internalize the 1.8-minute pace. Demanding you finish early is silly, but consistently running over time is disastrous.

    - **The Flag & Move On Method:** If a question completely stumps you after maybe 30-60 seconds of reading and thinking, or if you know it involves a rule you simply don't know, **make your best guess** (eliminate obvious wrong answers first!), **flag it** (if using computer software, or make a note on scratch paper), and **MOVE ON.** Do not—repeat, DO NOT—spend 5 minutes agonizing over one question. That's five minutes you could have used to answer two or three other questions you *did* know. It's simple math, folks. Wasting time on a lost cause is irrational.

    - **Batching Review (Optional):** Some find it helpful to return to flagged questions in batches (e.g., after finishing a block of 25 or 50 questions) rather than flipping back constantly. Experiment during practice to see if this works for you. The key is having a plan so you don't just randomly jump around.

    - **Time Checkpoints:** Know where you *should* be at certain points (e.g., after 30 mins, ~17 questions; after 1 hour, ~33 questions; halfway point – 1.5 hrs – 50 questions). If you're significantly behind, you need to consciously speed up slightly on the next few questions you feel confident about. Don't panic; just adjust rationally.

2. **Elimination is Your Best Friend:** Often, finding the *right* answer is less about certainty and more about definitively identifying the *wrong* answers. The MBE writers are masters of creating attractive distractors. Train yourself to spot them:

    - **Misstated Rule:** The answer choice sounds plausible but gets a key element of the legal rule wrong (e.g., confuses negligence per se with res ipsa loquitur). Knowing your black-letter law cold helps spot these.

    - **Facts Not in Evidence:** The answer choice relies on facts not present in the short hypo provided. Stick strictly to the facts given!

    - **Wrong Legal Standard/Test:** The answer applies the wrong level of scrutiny (Con Law), the wrong duty standard (Torts), or the wrong test for admissibility (Evidence).

    - **Correct Statement, Wrong Application:** The answer states a correct legal principle, but it doesn't actually apply to the specific facts or the question being asked.

    - **Too Broad or Too Narrow:** The answer uses absolute words like "always," "never," or is significantly broader or narrower than the issue presented. Be wary of extremes.

    - **Conclusory:** The answer just states a conclusion without implicit legal reasoning connected to the facts.

    - **The Process:** Actively cross out (mentally or physically on scratch paper) answer choices you identify as wrong. Often, you can confidently eliminate two choices quickly. Then, focus your analysis on the remaining two, re-reading the call of the question and the key facts to distinguish between them. Making an educated guess between two plausible options is far better than guessing randomly among four.

3. **Beware Common Traps:** The NCBE isn't necessarily trying to trick you maliciously, but they *are* testing your ability to read carefully and apply rules precisely. Watch out for:

- **The Call of the Question:** Read this FIRST and LAST. What *exactly* is being asked? Is it asking for the best argument for the plaintiff? The likely outcome? The correct legal reason for a ruling? Answering the wrong question—even with correct legal reasoning for something else—gets you zero points.
- **Red Herrings:** Irrelevant facts thrown into the hypo to distract you. Learn to filter these out and focus on the legally significant facts.
- **Double Negatives/Complex Phrasing:** Read carefully. Untangle the language to understand what the question and answer choices actually mean.
- **Assuming Facts Not Given:** Don't read into the hypo or assume missing information. Base your answer only on what's provided.
- **Ignoring Modifiers:** Words like "only," "unless," "except," "because" are critical. Missing them can completely change the meaning.

Scenario: Maria's MBE Shift

Maria initially approached MBE questions by trying to find the "right" answer immediately. She'd often get stuck between two choices, panic, and waste time. Her scores weren't improving. After focusing on elimination techniques during review (identifying why wrong answers were wrong), she shifted her approach. She started by actively looking for reasons to eliminate choices based on misstated rules or facts not in the hypo. This often left her with only one or two plausible options, making the final decision quicker and more accurate. She also became ruthless about the Flag & Move On method for questions she didn't immediately grasp, preventing herself from getting bogged down. Her scores started to climb, not because she magically learned more law overnight, but because she adopted a more rational process.

Essay Writing Mastery IRAC CRAC variations organization hitting key issues

Okay, you know the basic IRAC structure (Issue, Rule, Analysis, Conclusion). But writing high-scoring essays under time pressure requires more finesse. Graders aren't looking for beautiful prose; they're looking for efficient, organized legal analysis.

1. **Beyond Basic IRAC:** While IRAC is the foundation, think **CRAC** (Conclusion, Rule, Analysis, Conclusion) or **CREAC** (Conclusion, Rule, Explanation/Elaboration, Analysis, Conclusion).

- **Starting with the Conclusion (C):** Stating your conclusion upfront (e.g., "The court will likely find the defendant liable for negligence.") helps the grader immediately understand your position and follow your reasoning. It also forces *you* to take a position early.
- **Explaining the Rule (E):** Sometimes, especially with complex rules, briefly explaining the components or policy behind the rule *before* launching into the analysis can add clarity. Don't overdo this, but a short sentence can help.
- **The Second Conclusion (C):** Briefly restating the conclusion at the end provides closure for that specific issue.
- **Flexibility:** Don't be dogmatic. The key is clear structure. Use headings and subheadings liberally, especially for essays with multiple issues or parties. Break down complex analysis into smaller IRAC/CREAC units.

2. **Organization is King:** A disorganized essay, even with correct rules, is hard to grade and likely scores poorly.
    - **Outline First:** ALWAYS spend the first 3-5 minutes (yes, even within the 30-minute limit!) outlining your answer on scratch paper. Identify the major issues and sub-issues. Note the key rules and the critical facts you'll use for each. This roadmap prevents rambling and ensures you hit the main points. Trying to write "off the cuff" under pressure often leads to a jumbled mess. Resisting the outline because "I don't have time!" is irrational – it *saves* time by preventing rewrites and disorganized thinking.[1]
    - **Headings and Subheadings:** Use them! Simple headings like "Negligence Claim Against Driver" or subheadings like "I. Duty," "II. Breach," etc., make your answer vastly easier for the grader to follow and ensure you get credit for spotting the issues.
    - **One Issue per Paragraph (Generally):** Try to confine each distinct legal issue (or sub-issue) to its own paragraph or series of paragraphs, applying the IRAC/CREAC structure within that section.[2]
3. **Hitting Key Issues & Analysis:** Graders have checklists. They're looking for specific things.

- **Spot the Major Issues:** Don't get lost in minor details. Focus on the big legal questions raised by the facts. Your outline helps prioritize these.
- **State the Rule Accurately:** Use the correct legal terminology. Don't paraphrase loosely. Black-letter law precision matters.
- **ANALYSIS IS KEY:** This is where points are often made or lost. Don't just state a rule and jump to a conclusion. **Explicitly apply the rule to the specific facts.** Use phrases like "Here, the fact that [X happened] demonstrates that the defendant breached his duty because..." or "Unlike the rule requires, the plaintiff did [Y], therefore..." Weave the legally relevant facts into your application of the rule. This shows the grader you understand *how* the rule works in practice. Avoid conclusory statements like "Therefore, there was a breach." Show *why*.
- **Address Both Sides (If Appropriate):** For some issues, briefly acknowledging counterarguments or alternative analyses can show a deeper understanding, but don't spend too much time on this unless the call of the question requires it. Focus on reaching a reasoned conclusion.

Scenario: Kevin's Essay Evolution

Kevin's early practice essays were disorganized walls of text. He knew the rules but struggled to present them clearly under time pressure. He resisted outlining, thinking it wasted time. His grader feedback consistently mentioned "poor organization" and "conclusory analysis." Kevin finally forced himself to use the 3-5 minute outline method. He also started using CRAC and incorporating simple headings. Suddenly, his practice essays became much clearer. He also focused deliberately on the Analysis step, forcing himself to connect rules to specific facts using "because" or "since." His self-graded scores improved markedly, mainly due to better structure and more explicit analysis, even if his underlying rule knowledge hadn't changed dramatically.

MPT Domination Deconstructing the file and library outlining time management

The MPT often terrifies people because it seems unpredictable. But it's actually testing a specific, learnable *skill set*. It's not about recalling law; it's about acting like a junior lawyer given a task, a pile of documents, and a deadline.

1. **Deconstructing the File & Library Efficiently:** You don't have time to read every word passively. You need a system. (Refer back to the 45/45 strategy in Chapter 8/Week 5).

    - **Task Memo First (5 min):** Read this *very* carefully. What is your role? Who is the audience? What specific document must you produce (objective memo, persuasive brief, client letter, etc.)? What tone is required? What specific legal issues or questions should you address? This memo is your primary instruction set – ignore it at your peril!

    - **Skim Library & File (5-10 min):** Quickly look at the headings, case names, statute titles in the Library. Glance at the types of documents in the File (interview notes, emails, contracts, etc.). Get a sense of the legal area and the key documents *before* reading deeply.

    - **Active Reading (25-30 min):** Read the Library first (often helpful to know the rules before the facts) or the File first (your preference, experiment in practice), but read *actively*. Highlight/note relevant legal rules, key facts (pro and con, if applicable), specific instructions, deadlines, client objectives, etc. Constantly ask: "How does this relate to the Task Memo's requirements?"

2. **Outlining is Non-Negotiable:** As with essays, you *must* create an outline during that first 45-minute block. Trying to write an MPT directly from the documents without an outline is practically guaranteed to result in a disorganized, incomplete mess.

    - **Structure Follows Task:** Your outline structure should directly mirror the document requested in the Task Memo. If it asks for an objective memo with sections for Introduction, Legal Analysis, and Conclusion, your outline needs those headings. If it's a persuasive brief needing specific point headings, outline those.

    - **Integrate File & Library:** Under each outline heading, jot down the key rules from the Library and the supporting/contradicting facts from the File. Think IRAC/CREAC even here – Issue (from Task Memo/Facts), Rule (from Library), Analysis (connecting Library rules to File facts), Conclusion (addressing the issue).

- **Be Detailed Enough:** Your outline should be more than just headings; it needs the substance (key facts/rules) to guide your writing.

3. **Time Management Refinements (Within the 45/45):**
   - **Don't Get Stuck Reading:** If one case or statute seems overly complex or confusing, grasp the main point and move on. You likely don't need every nuance.
   - **Prioritize:** Focus on the issues explicitly mentioned in the Task Memo. Don't go down rabbit holes on interesting but irrelevant side issues.
   - **Allocate Writing Time:** Within the second 45 minutes, mentally allocate time for each section of your outline. If you have three main arguments, maybe allow ~12 minutes each, plus time for intro/conclusion/polish. Stick to these mini-deadlines as best you can.
   - **Write Concisely:** Use clear, direct language. Avoid lengthy block quotes unless absolutely necessary. Get straight to the point. Graders value clarity and responsiveness to the task over flowery language.
   - **Finish!** It's better to have a complete, reasonably organized answer addressing all parts of the Task Memo, even if slightly rough, than a perfectly polished but incomplete answer. Aim to get words down for every part of your outline.

Scenario: Sarah's MPT Turnaround

Sarah initially panicked during MPT practice. She'd try to read everything thoroughly, run out of time, and start writing frantically without a plan. Her practice scores were poor. She then committed to the 45/45 strategy and focused on active reading linked directly to the Task Memo. The biggest change was forcing herself to create a detailed outline within the first 45 minutes, mapping Library rules and File facts to the required structure before writing. This felt slow at first, but she found that writing the second half was much faster and more organized because she had a clear roadmap. Her ability to finish the MPTs improved dramatically, as did her scores, because she was finally producing a complete and responsive work product.

Mastering these components isn't about sudden flashes of brilliance. It's about understanding the mechanics of each section, adopting rational strategies, practicing those strategies deliberately, and refining them based on feedback.[3] It's work, but it's focused work that yields results.

Sharpening Your Tools

Knowing the law is like having the raw materials. Knowing basic IRAC or MPT format is like having a basic hammer and saw. The advanced techniques discussed here are about sharpening those tools – learning to use the hammer more effectively, the saw more precisely. Applying strategies for timing, elimination, organization, and targeted analysis allows you to build a much better final product, especially under the severe time constraints of the bar exam. Don't just passively read about these techniques; actively incorporate them into your remaining practice and review. The next step is understanding how to learn most effectively *from* that practice.

Key Takeaways for Chapter 13

- **MBE:** Use strict timing (Flag & Move On), systematic elimination of wrong answer choices (spotting misstated rules, wrong facts, etc.), and awareness of common traps (call of the question, red herrings) to improve efficiency and accuracy.
- **Essays:** Employ structured formats like CRAC/CREAC, always outline first (3-5 mins), use headings, and focus on explicit Analysis (connecting rules to specific facts) to make answers clear and responsive for graders.
- **MPT:** Deconstruct the File and Library efficiently using the Task Memo as your guide (e.g., 45/45 strategy), create a detailed outline integrating rules and facts *before* writing, and manage time strictly during the writing phase to ensure a complete, responsive answer.
- These techniques are rational tools requiring deliberate practice, not magic bullets guaranteeing perfection. Focus on process improvement.

Chapter 14: Learning from Practice - Analyzing Performance

You've been practicing diligently, following the schedule, maybe even incorporating some of the advanced techniques from the last chapter. Good. But are you truly *learning* from that practice? Many bar applicants spend countless hours doing practice questions and exams but fail to extract the full educational value from them. They equate *doing* practice with *learning* from practice, which is often flat-out wrong. Effective learning requires **deliberate analysis and reflection** on your performance, especially your mistakes.[4] Furthermore, using data from full simulated exams and ongoing practice to **rationally adapt** your study focus is essential for efficient preparation. Simply churning through questions without deep review or adaptation is like running on a hamster wheel – lots of motion, not much progress. Let's break down how to make your practice actually count.

The Power of Simulated Exams Why full length practice matters

In Week 6 (and perhaps again later), this schedule includes a full simulated exam. Some people resist this, thinking, "Why waste two whole days? I could be learning more rules!" or "It's too stressful! I'll just do short practice sets." This thinking, while understandable if you fear discomfort, misses the unique and irreplaceable benefits of full-length simulation:

1. **Stamina and Endurance:** The real bar exam is a two-day mental marathon. Can you maintain focus and analytical rigor for six hours straight, two days in a row? Short practice sets don't replicate this demand. Full simulations build mental endurance and expose energy flags you wouldn't otherwise notice.[5] Knowing you *can* physically and mentally survive the duration builds confidence.

2. **Timing Under Pressure:** It's one thing to manage time in a 30-minute essay or a 60-minute MBE set. It's entirely different to manage pacing across a 3-hour MPT session or a 3-hour, 100-question MBE block, especially when fatigue sets in. Simulations reveal how your timing holds up (or falls apart) under realistic, sustained pressure.

3. **Simulating Exam Day Conditions:** Simulations allow you to practice your entire exam day routine: wake-up time, breakfast, travel (if practicing elsewhere), managing breaks, dealing with potential distractions, and handling the anxiety

that comes with a high-stakes environment. It desensitizes you somewhat to the process.

4. **Revealing Hidden Weaknesses:** Some knowledge or skill gaps only become apparent during longer sessions. Maybe you realize your Contracts knowledge is solid for 30 minutes but fades after two hours. Maybe your essay organization deteriorates significantly by the fifth essay. Simulations provide a more accurate diagnostic of your *functional* knowledge and skills under exam conditions.[6]

5. **Feedback Goldmine:** The sheer volume of data generated by a full simulated exam (200 MBEs, 6+ essays, 2 MPTs) provides a rich, integrated picture of your strengths and weaknesses across all subjects and skills, allowing for highly targeted review and adaptation (more on this below).

Thinking you can adequately prepare for a marathon by only running short sprints is illogical. Simulations are necessary dress rehearsals that provide feedback you simply cannot get any other way.[7] Don't avoid them because they feel hard or you fear the results. Embrace them as learning opportunities.

Effective Answer Review Going Beyond Right Wrong

This is arguably the **single most important learning activity** in bar prep, yet it's the one most often skipped or rushed due to impatience or ego-defense ("I don't want to dwell on my mistakes!"). Simply seeing your score or checking if an answer was right or wrong is almost useless. **Deep review is where the learning happens.**

MBE Review Technique:

- **For Incorrect Answers:**

    1. **Why was my choice wrong?** Specifically identify the flaw. Was it a misstated rule? Facts not in hypo? Wrong legal test? Too broad/narrow? Read the explanation carefully.

    2. **Why is the correct answer right?** Understand the legal reasoning and how it applies to the specific facts. Don't just accept it; make sure you *understand* the logic.

    3. **What was the specific rule I missed or misapplied?** Look up that rule in your outline immediately. Review it. Maybe make a flashcard.

4. **Did I misread the Call or the Facts?** Be honest. Many errors come from simple reading comprehension mistakes under pressure. Note this pattern if it occurs.

5. **Was it a time pressure mistake?** Did you rush and pick impulsively? Acknowledge this.

- **For Correct Answers:** Don't just skip them! Briefly review *why* your answer was correct. Did you get it right for the right reasons? Or did you just guess luckily? Reinforcing the correct reasoning helps solidify your understanding.

- **Keep an Error Log (Optional but helpful):** Briefly note down rules you consistently miss or types of errors you make (e.g., "Keep mixing up battery/assault elements," "Tend to misread facts on Negligence questions," "Always get Rule Against Perpetuities wrong"—join the club!). Reviewing this log periodically highlights patterns.

Essay Review Technique:

1. **Read the Model Answer/Grading Rubric First:** Understand what issues the graders were looking for and the key rules and facts they expected.

2. **Compare Your Answer Issue by Issue:**

   - **Issue Spotting:** Did you spot all the major issues identified in the model? Did you discuss non-issues?

   - **Rule Statements:** Compare your rule statements word-for-word (or nearly) with the model. Were yours accurate? Complete? Did you state the relevant exceptions or elements?

   - **Analysis (Application):** This is crucial. Did the model answer use specific facts to support its analysis that you missed or ignored? Did you just state conclusions, while the model showed *how* the rule applied to the facts? How did your reasoning differ?

   - **Organization:** Was your IRAC/CREAC structure as clear as the model's? Did you use headings effectively?

3. **Self-Grade Honestly:** Give yourself an estimated score based on the comparison. Be tougher rather than easier. Where did you likely lose the most points? Why?

4. **Note Deficiencies:** Write down specific weaknesses (e.g., "Missed discussion of comparative fault," "Rule statement for agency authority was incomplete," "Failed to use key facts X and Y in analysis"). Use this for targeted review later.

MPT Review Technique:

1. **Review the Model Answer & Point Sheet:** Understand the expected format, tone, organization, key issues, relevant rules (from the Library), and critical facts (from the File).

2. **Assess Task Compliance:** Did you follow the Task Memo instructions precisely? Did you produce the correct document type with the required sections/headings? Was the tone appropriate (objective/persuasive)?

3. **Evaluate File/Library Use:** Did you effectively extract the key facts needed? Did you correctly identify and apply the relevant legal rules provided in the Library? Did you ignore irrelevant information?

4. **Analyze Organization & Analysis:** Was your structure logical and easy to follow? Was your reasoning sound? Did you connect the rules to the facts effectively? For persuasive tasks, was your argument convincing? For objective tasks, was it balanced?

5. **Check Timing & Completeness:** Were you able to complete the task (or most of it) within the time limit? Where did your timing strategy succeed or fail?

6. **Note Skill Gaps:** Identify specific MPT skills needing improvement (e.g., "Need to outline faster," "Struggle with organizing persuasive arguments," "Tend to miss key facts buried in exhibits").

Devoting **significant, dedicated time** to this kind of deep review after every practice session or simulation is absolutely essential. Rushing this step means you're likely just repeating the same mistakes. Challenging the irrational belief "Reviewing mistakes is unpleasant, so I should avoid it" is central to effective learning. Accept the discomfort as a necessary part of getting better.

Adapting Your Study Based on Performance Data

Your practice results—MBE scores broken down by subject, essay self-grades, MPT assessments, simulation performance—provide invaluable **data**. Ignoring this data and just blindly sticking to a generic plan is inefficient. You need to use this information to **rationally adapt** your study focus, especially in the later weeks.

How to Adapt Rationally:

1. **Identify Clear Patterns:** Don't overreact to one bad score on a single practice set. Look for **consistent patterns** over time and across different practice types. Is Civil Procedure *always* your lowest MBE score? Do you *consistently* miss issue X on Torts essays? Is MPT timing *always* a problem?
2. **Prioritize Based on Impact:** Focus your adaptation efforts on weaknesses that will likely have the **biggest impact** on your score. A subject tested heavily on both MBE and essays (like Contracts or Torts) where you are weak deserves more attention than an obscure, rarely tested MEE topic you find difficult. Weakness in a core skill like MBE timing or essay analysis needs more focus than struggling with one specific niche rule.
3. **Make Specific, Targeted Adjustments:** Don't just vaguely "study weak areas more." Make specific changes to how you allocate your time within the existing schedule framework:
    - **Allocate Review Time:** During your scheduled evening review blocks or weekend review, consciously spend *more* time reviewing rules and doing practice problems related to your identified weak areas.
    - **Select Practice Problems Strategically:** When doing mixed MBE sets, make sure to include extra questions from weak subjects. Choose essay prompts specifically targeting weak areas. Practice MPTs focusing on skill gaps (e.g., do more persuasive briefs if that's your weakness).
    - **Revisit Foundational Material:** Sometimes weakness stems from a shaky understanding of basics. Briefly revisit your core outline or lecture material for that specific weak topic, then immediately apply it with practice questions.
4. **Don't Abandon Strengths Entirely:** While focusing on weaknesses, don't completely neglect subjects or skills where you are strong. Continue including

them in mixed practice to maintain proficiency. The goal is balance, weighted towards improvement where it's needed most.

5. **Track Your Adjustments:** Briefly note what changes you're making and periodically assess if they seem to be helping (based on subsequent practice data, not just feelings). Be prepared to adjust again if needed.

Avoiding Irrational Adaptation:

- **Don't Panic Based on Feelings:** Don't drastically change your plan just because you *feel* anxious or had one bad day. Base decisions on objective data patterns.
- **Don't Chase Perfection:** Don't spend excessive time trying to get one difficult subject from 60% to 65% if it means neglecting another subject stuck at 40%. Aim for competence across the board.
- **Don't Compare Obsessively:** Hearing that someone else is scoring higher doesn't mean you need to copy their (possibly irrational) study methods. Focus on *your* data and *your* plan.

Using performance data to guide your study is simply smart work. It allows you to direct your limited time and energy where it will likely yield the greatest return.

Making Mistakes Work For You

Mistakes and subpar performance in practice are not signs of impending doom; they are **feedback**. Invaluable, essential feedback. The irrational response is to fear mistakes, avoid reviewing them, or let them convince you you're inadequate. The rational response is to *welcome* mistakes made *during practice* as opportunities. Opportunities to identify rule gaps, refine skills, understand question patterns, and adjust your strategy.[8] By embracing thorough review and using performance data to guide your efforts, you turn those inevitable errors from sources of frustration into engines of learning and improvement. This analytical approach is crucial as you head into the final, critical phase of preparation.

Key Takeaways for Chapter 14

- Full simulated exams are necessary for building stamina, practicing timing under sustained pressure, simulating exam conditions, and revealing weaknesses not apparent in shorter practice sets.
- Effective answer review is critical for learning and goes far beyond checking right/wrong.
- **MBE Review:** Analyze *why* wrong answers are wrong and right answers are right; identify specific rule gaps or error types (reading, time).
- **Essay Review:** Compare structure, issue spotting, rule statements, and factual analysis against model answers/rubrics; self-grade honestly.
- **MPT Review:** Assess task compliance, effective use of File/Library, organization, analysis, and timing strategy against model answers/point sheets.
- Use performance data (scores, error patterns, self-assessments) to identify **consistent weak areas**.[9]
- **Rationally adapt** your study plan by making specific, targeted adjustments to focus more review and practice time on high-impact weaknesses, without completely neglecting strengths.
- Avoid emotional reactions or perfectionistic demands when reviewing performance; treat mistakes as feedback and data as a guide.

Chapter 15: The Final Week - Countdown to Exam Day

You've arrived at the final week. After seven weeks of intensive, structured study, simulation, and targeted practice, the exam looms large. This week is **different**. It's not about cramming massive amounts of information or putting in brutally long hours – doing so now is more likely to cause burnout and anxiety than actual benefit. Instead, Week 8 (as scheduled in Chapter 12) is about **final polishing, meticulous logistical planning, and crucially, managing your mindset.** The primary battle now is often internal: fighting the rising tide of anxiety, the catastrophic "what ifs," and the irrational urge to either study yourself into exhaustion or give up in despair. Your goal is to arrive at Day 1 feeling as prepared, calm, and confident as realistically possible, focusing on what you *can* control in these final days.

What to Do and NOT Do in the Last 7 Days

Resist the panic-driven urge to completely overhaul your approach or dramatically increase study time. Follow the tapered schedule outlined in Chapter 12. Here's a recap of the core principles:

What TO Do:

1. **Light Review & Active Memorization:** Focus on reviewing your personalized attack outlines, checklists, flashcards, or notes on frequently confused rules or your identified weak areas. Keep it *light* and *active* (e.g., reciting rules aloud, rewriting frameworks from memory). Aim for consolidation, not new learning.

2. **Confirm ALL Logistics:** Double- and triple-check everything related to exam day: admission ticket printed? Valid ID ready? Laptop charged and tested (with backup power if allowed/needed)? Exam location and travel route confirmed? Parking sorted? Start/end times and break times noted? Site rules on food/drink/bags/electronics understood? Packing list finalized (see below)? Leave nothing to chance; logistical snafus cause unnecessary stress.

3. **Practice Stress Management DAILY:** Intentionally use techniques that work for you – deep breathing, short meditations, visualization (seeing yourself handle the exam calmly), listening to calming music, light exercise like walking. Make this a scheduled part of your day.

4. **Challenge Negative Thoughts ACTIVELY:** Your brain *will* likely bombard you with "what ifs" and self-doubt. Don't just let them run rampant. Identify the

irrational beliefs ("I *must* know everything," "If I feel anxious, I'll fail," "Forgetting one rule is a disaster") and actively dispute them with rational counter-statements ("I've prepared thoroughly," "Anxiety is normal and I can function with it," "I don't need perfection, just competence," "I will focus on what I *can* control").

5. **Prioritize Sleep:** Seriously. Aim for 7-9 hours per night. Consistent sleep is far more valuable now than extra hours staring bleary-eyed at an outline. Follow good sleep hygiene (dark room, cool temperature, avoid screens before bed). Don't catastrophize one poor night – your body can cope, but aim for consistency.

6. **Eat Well & Hydrate:** Fuel your brain and body properly.[10] Avoid excessive sugar, caffeine, or heavy foods that might make you feel sluggish or jittery. Drink plenty of water.

7. **Light Physical Activity:** Gentle movement like walking can significantly reduce stress and improve mood.[11] Don't start an intense new workout regime, but don't become completely sedentary either.

8. **Plan Your Taper:** Follow the schedule reducing study hours significantly by mid-week, with very little required the day before the exam. Trust that the work has been done.

What NOT To Do:

1. **NO Heavy Cramming:** Trying to learn new subjects or deep-dive into complex topics now is likely futile and anxiety-provoking. Stick to light review.

2. **NO Full Practice Exams (Generally):** Unless you took your last one early in Week 7 and feel a *very* strong need for one final run-through *early* this week (like Monday), avoid full-length simulations. They take significant time and mental energy, and a potentially discouraging score now can wreck your confidence. Shorter, targeted practice early in the week is the most you should consider.

3. **DON'T Sacrifice Sleep for Study:** Absolutely counterproductive. Sleep consolidates memory and restores cognitive function.[12] Protect it.

4. **DON'T Engage with Panicked Peers:** Avoid conversations (online or in person) with fellow test-takers who are spiraling into anxiety, comparing notes frantically, or debating obscure rules. Protect your mental space.
5. **DON'T Make Major Changes:** Don't suddenly change your diet, sleep schedule, study methods, or start taking new supplements. Stick with what's been working.
6. **DON'T Over-Rely on Caffeine/Stimulants:** While moderate caffeine might be part of your routine, dramatically increasing intake now can worsen anxiety, disrupt sleep, and lead to crashes.
7. **DON'T Study the Night Before (or morning of):** Your brain needs rest. Trust your preparation. At most, a 15-30 minute glance at key checklists *if it calms you*, but nothing more.

Logistics Planning Travel hotel packing list exam site rules

Smooth logistics minimize exam-day stress. Thinking "Logistics are minor, I'll figure it out later" is foolishly risking unnecessary panic when you can least afford it.

The Checklist:

- **Identification:** Do you have the specific, valid, non-expired government-issued photo ID required by your jurisdiction? Check the name matches your admission ticket *exactly*. Have a backup ID if possible.
- **Admission Ticket/Materials:** Print it out. Read all instructions on it. Note your assigned seat number if applicable.
- **Travel Plan:** How are you getting to the test center each day? Driving? Public transport? Ride-sharing? Walking?
  - **Confirm Route:** Know exactly where you're going. Do a test drive during rush hour if possible.
  - **Confirm Timing:** How long will it take? Allow **plenty** of extra time for traffic, parking, security lines. Aim to arrive early, but not *so* early you have hours to sit and fret.
  - **Parking:** Where will you park? Is it paid? Do you need cash/card/app? Have a backup parking plan.

    - **Hotel (If Applicable):** Confirm reservation. Plan travel between hotel and test center. Check hotel amenities (quiet room? reliable wake-up call?).
- **Packing List - The Essentials (Check YOUR jurisdiction's rules - they vary!):**
    - **Required:** ID, admission ticket.
    - **Laptop Examinees:** Laptop, power cord, mouse (if used), keyboard (if used/allowed), ensure exam software is installed, tested, and updated. Maybe backup power source if allowed?
    - **Writing Supplies (If needed/allowed):** Pens (multiple working ones!), pencils, highlighters. Check specific rules on types/colors.
    - **Comfort:** Comfortable, layered clothing (rooms can be freezing or hot), glasses/contacts (plus spares/solution), tissues.
    - **Health:** Any necessary medications (check rules on bringing them in), feminine hygiene products, basic pain reliever (again, check rules). Earplugs (highly recommended, even if provided, bring your own preferred type). Maybe an eye mask for breaks.
    - **Sustenance (Check rules STRICTLY):** Water bottle (often must be clear, label removed), quiet snacks for breaks (protein bars, nuts, fruit – avoid noisy wrappers!), planned lunch (if bringing your own). Wallet/keys. Watch (non-smartwatch, if allowed, for pacing).
- **What NOT to Bring (Check rules STRICTLY):** Cell phone (usually must be completely off and stored away), smartwatch, study materials, notes, books, unauthorized calculators, weapons, noisy items, strong perfumes/colognes. **Violation of rules can lead to dismissal from the exam.** Don't risk it!
- **Exam Site Rules:** Re-read all rules about check-in procedures, security, allowed items, break policies, restroom usage, technical support for laptops, emergency procedures. Know what to expect.

Scenario: Chloe's Calm Arrival

Chloe was naturally anxious. Instead of letting logistics add to her stress, she meticulously planned Week 8, Day 1. She confirmed her hotel near the test center.

She test-drove the route on Tuesday morning. She packed her clear ziplock bag with ID, ticket, pens, earplugs, medication, and approved snacks on Wednesday. She laid out her layered outfit. On exam morning, she simply executed her pre-planned routine: wake up, eat breakfast, grab her bag, travel the known route, park in the designated area, and walk into the center calmly, arriving 45 minutes early as planned. While still nervous about the test itself, she experienced zero stress about logistics because she had rationally controlled that variable in advance.

Cultivating Calm and Confidence

This is where you actively manage your thinking. Confidence isn't about *knowing* you'll pass; it's about trusting your *preparation* and your *ability to handle the process*.[13] Calm isn't about *feeling* zero anxiety; it's about *functioning effectively despite* the anxiety.

Strategies:

1. **Rational Self-Talk:** Continuously challenge negative and catastrophic thoughts.[14] Replace "I'm going to fail" with "I have prepared thoroughly and will do my best; the outcome is uncertain, but I can handle it." Replace "I must feel calm" with "Feeling anxious is normal before a big event; I can accept this feeling and still focus on my strategy." Write down some rational coping statements and read them daily.

2. **Focus on Process, Not Outcome:** You cannot control the score. You *can* control whether you follow your timing strategy, whether you outline your essays, whether you use elimination techniques, whether you manage your breaks effectively. Focus your mental energy on executing the *process* you've practiced.

3. **Review Your Effort:** Remind yourself of the weeks of structured work you've completed. You didn't just passively read; you did thousands of MBE questions, wrote dozens of essays, practiced MPTs, reviewed mistakes. Acknowledge this effort – it's the basis for rational confidence.

4. **Visualization:** Spend a few minutes each day visualizing yourself navigating the exam days successfully – arriving calmly, managing time effectively, handling difficult questions without panic, using breaks well, feeling focused. Make the visualization realistic, including acknowledging potential nerves but seeing yourself cope with them.

5. **Acceptance:** Radically accept the situation. The exam is difficult. You might feel anxious. You might not know every answer. You might make mistakes. *Accepting* these realities reduces the struggle against them, freeing up mental energy to perform. Fighting reality ("It *shouldn't* be this hard!" "I *must not* feel nervous!") is exhausting and futile.

6. **Draw on Past Resilience:** You've overcome challenges before (getting into/through law school, for instance!). Remind yourself of your ability to handle difficult situations.

Confidence isn't puffed-up arrogance; it's a quiet belief in your preparation and your ability to cope. Calm isn't absence of nerves; it's the ability to function effectively alongside them. Cultivate these through rational thinking and deliberate practice this week.

Controlling the Controllables

The final week is less about inputting knowledge and more about outputting readiness – logistical, mental, and emotional. You can't control the exam questions, the grading, or the final result. Fretting endlessly about those uncontrollable is a recipe for misery. What you *can* control is your preparation this week: light review, meticulous logistics planning, prioritizing rest, and actively managing your mindset through rational self-talk and stress reduction techniques. Pour your energy into those controllable factors. Trust the weeks of work behind you. Walk into that exam room knowing you did everything reasonably possible to prepare not just your knowledge base, but your entire self for the challenge ahead. The next chapter focuses on executing during the exam days themselves.

Key Takeaways for Chapter 15

- The final week focuses on light review/memorization, logistics, stress management, and rest – NOT heavy cramming.[15]
- **DO:** Light active review, confirm all logistics meticulously, practice stress management daily, actively challenge negative thoughts, prioritize sleep and health, taper study hours.
- **DON'T:** Cram new material, take late full practice exams, sacrifice sleep, engage with panicked peers, make major routine changes.

- Create a detailed logistics plan and checklist covering ID, tickets, travel, packing (check rules!), and site procedures to minimize exam-day stress.
- Cultivate functional calm and confidence through rational self-talk, focusing on the controllable process (not the uncontrollable outcome), reviewing past effort, visualization, and acceptance of anxiety.[16]
- Avoid studying the night before the exam; prioritize rest and mental calm.

Chapter 16: Conquering the Exam Days

The preparation is done. The countdown is over. It's showtime. These next two (or possibly three, depending on your jurisdiction) days are the culmination of your efforts. While the outcome is uncertain, your *approach* to navigating these days is firmly within your control. This chapter provides a practical guide for executing your plan under pressure, managing inevitable nerves and challenges, and maximizing your performance by focusing on strategy and resilience. Thinking you *must* feel perfectly calm or perform flawlessly is irrational; aiming to implement your strategies effectively and handle difficulties rationally *is* achievable.

Day Of Strategy Morning routine managing nerves

How you start the day can significantly impact your mindset and performance. Consistency and calm are the goals.

1. **The Wake-Up:** Use multiple alarms if needed. Wake up early enough for a calm, unhurried routine – don't hit snooze until the last second and rush frantically.

2. **Fuel Up Sensibly:** Eat the breakfast you planned – something with protein and complex carbohydrates for sustained energy (e.g., oatmeal, eggs, whole-wheat toast). Avoid sugary cereals or pastries that lead to a crash.[17] Hydrate, but don't overdo liquids right before leaving. Take any regular medications.

3. **Mindset Moment:** Take 5-10 minutes for your chosen calming practice – deep breathing, briefly reviewing rational coping statements ("I am prepared," "I can handle anxiety," "Focus on one question at a time"), or positive visualization. Set your intention for the day: to stay focused and execute your strategies.

4. **Final Logistics Check:** Grab your packed exam bag, ID, ticket. Dress in your comfortable, layered clothing.

5. **Travel Time:** Leave according to your pre-planned schedule, allowing ample buffer time. Listen to calming music or silence during the commute – avoid frantic news radio or last-minute podcasts about law.

6. **Arrival at the Center:** Arrive with enough time to park, go through security, find your room/seat, and use the restroom without rushing (aim for maybe 30-45 minutes early, adjust based on your center's procedures).[18]

7. **Managing Pre-Exam Nerves:** It's normal to feel butterflies, maybe even nausea. Accept these physical sensations. Use deep, slow breaths. Avoid congregating with highly anxious test-takers engaging in last-minute panicked discussions ("Did you study X? I heard Y is definitely tested!"). Find a quiet spot, focus on your breathing, perhaps review your key strategy points mentally (e.g., "45/45 on MPT," "Outline essays," "Flag & Move On for MBE"). Remind yourself: **Nerves mean you care, they don't mean you're unprepared or doomed.** You can perform well even while feeling anxious.

During the Exam Timing checkpoints handling difficult questions staying focused

Once the clock starts, execution is key.

1. **Timing, Timing, Timing:** This is paramount.
   - **Internal Clock:** Be acutely aware of the time limits for each section (e.g., 90 mins/MPT, 30 mins/Essay, 1.8 mins/MBE question).
   - **Checkpoints:** Use predetermined checkpoints. For MBE, know how many questions you should have completed by the 30, 60, 90-minute marks etc. For essays/MPTs, mentally allocate time for outlining vs. writing and stick to it.
   - **If You Fall Behind:** Don't panic! Take a deep breath. Identify an opportunity to catch up slightly on the *next* few questions/tasks you feel more confident about. Do NOT rush wildly through everything – that leads to more errors. Make small, conscious adjustments to your pace.
   - **If You Finish Early:** Use the extra time wisely. On MBE, review flagged questions or reconsider answers you were very unsure about (but be cautious about changing answers unless you have a clear reason!). On essays/MPTs, proofread for glaring errors, check if you addressed all parts of the prompt, ensure rules are stated accurately. Don't just sit there or leave early!
2. **Handling Difficult Questions/Tasks:** You *will* encounter questions or prompts that seem impossible or confusing. How you handle them is critical.
   - **MBE:** If a question stumps you, apply your elimination strategy. Remove obviously wrong answers. Make your best educated guess

among the remaining options. **Flag it and MOVE ON.** Do not allow one hard question to steal time from several easier ones. It's irrational to demand you know everything.

- **Essays:** If an essay topic seems unfamiliar or you blank on the specific rule, don't leave it blank! Do your best: Identify the likely legal area. State a general, related rule if you can't recall the specific one. Apply the facts logically to that general rule. Make arguments based on policy or fairness if appropriate. Spotting the major issue and attempting a structured analysis, even with an imperfect rule, often earns more points than a blank page or a panicked ramble. Structure (IRAC/CREAC) can save you even when knowledge falters.

- **MPT:** If the task seems bizarre or the law is dense, focus first on the **Task Memo**. What absolutely *must* you produce? Then, tackle the Library for the core rules and the File for the key facts related *specifically* to that task. Stick to your timing strategy (45/45). Even a basically structured answer that directly addresses the Task Memo using *some* relevant facts and rules is better than getting lost and producing nothing coherent.

3. **Staying Focused:** Distractions (internal and external) are inevitable.

    - **External Distractions:** Use your earplugs! Tune out coughs, shuffling papers, proctor announcements (unless directed at you). Keep your eyes on your own work.

    - **Internal Distractions:** If your mind wanders ("What if I fail?" "What's for lunch?" "Did I leave the stove on?"), gently but firmly bring your focus back to the **current task**. "Okay, back to question 73." "Focus on outlining this essay issue." Deep breaths can help reset focus.[19]

    - **Task Concentration:** Train yourself to think only about the question, essay, or MPT section directly in front of you. Don't worry about how you did on the last section or how hard the next one might be. Be present.

Scenario: David's Mid-MBE Save

During the morning MBE session, David hit a string of five questions on Real Property future interests that completely bewildered him. He felt panic rising, thinking "I'm blowing it! I don't know anything!" Instead of freezing, he employed his strategy: For each of the five, he quickly eliminated the answers he felt were definitely wrong, made his best guess between the remaining two, flagged them, and moved on, forcing himself not to spend more than 1.5 minutes on each. This felt awful in the moment. But by moving on, he saved crucial time and was able to answer the subsequent questions (which were on subjects he knew better) calmly and accurately. He accepted he wouldn't get every question right and focused on maximizing points where he could, rather than demanding perfect knowledge and letting the hard questions derail him.

Between Sessions Days Resetting and recovering

How you use the breaks and the evening between exam days is just as important as how you perform during the timed sessions.

1. **Lunch Breaks:**
    - **Physically Leave:** Get out of the exam room and, if possible, the building. Fresh air helps.
    - **Refuel:** Eat the sensible lunch and snacks you packed. Hydrate.
    - **NO Post-Mortem:** Absolutely **do NOT discuss morning questions** with anyone. It serves zero purpose, often spreads misinformation, and fuels anxiety. If people try, politely excuse yourself: "I need to clear my head."
    - **Mental Reset:** Don't think about the exam. Listen to music, meditate briefly, stretch, focus on your breathing. Prepare mentally for the afternoon session as a fresh start.
2. **Evening Between Day 1 and Day 2:**
    - **COMPLETE Shutdown:** Once you leave the test center after Day 1, **consider your exam-related work DONE for the day.**
    - **NO Debriefing:** Do not analyze how you think you did. Do not talk about specific questions with anyone. Your perception is likely inaccurate anyway, and it's counterproductive.

- **NO Studying:** Do NOT crack open your outlines or do practice questions trying to "make up" for perceived weaknesses on Day 1. This will likely increase anxiety and tire you out for Day 2, yielding negligible benefit. Trust your preparation.
- **Recovery Routine:** Eat a satisfying, healthy dinner. Engage in a relaxing, non-law-related activity (watch a movie, talk to a supportive friend about anything *but* the exam, read a light novel). Prepare your logistics for Day 2 (pack lunch, lay out clothes). Get to bed at a reasonable hour, prioritizing rest even if sleep is difficult due to nerves.

3. **After the Final Session:**
   - **Acknowledge Completion:** You did it! Walk out, take a deep breath, and congratulate yourself for getting through the entire ordeal.
   - **Resist Immediate Debrief:** Avoid the crowds dissecting questions immediately outside the test center. Head home or to your hotel.
   - **Plan Your Recovery:** Have a plan for the evening and the next few days focused on rest, relaxation, and reconnecting with normal life. See the Conclusion chapter for more on this.

Managing the "in-between" times effectively by prioritizing mental reset and recovery prevents Day 1 difficulties or anxieties from poisoning Day 2 performance. It requires discipline to resist the urge to rehash or cram, but it's a rational strategy for maintaining peak performance over the duration.

Executing Under Pressure And Surviving

The bar exam isn't just a test of legal knowledge; it's a test of performance under pressure, endurance, and emotional regulation.[20] Success often comes down to executing well-rehearsed strategies – managing time, handling difficult questions rationally (guess and move on!), staying focused, and using breaks effectively to reset. You prepared not just the 'what' (the law) but the 'how' (the strategies). By focusing on implementing those strategies, accepting inevitable challenges without catastrophizing, and prioritizing recovery between sessions, you gave yourself the best possible chance to demonstrate your competence. You survived the gauntlet. Now, give yourself permission to recover fully.

Key Takeaways for Chapter 16

- Establish a calm, consistent morning routine on exam days, prioritizing sensible nutrition, hydration, and brief relaxation/mindset exercises.
- Manage pre-exam nerves upon arrival by accepting them as normal, using deep breathing, and avoiding panicked discussions with peers.
- During the exam, strictly adhere to timing strategies and checkpoints; handle difficult questions by eliminating, guessing, flagging (optional), and **moving on** quickly.
- Practice task concentration, gently bringing focus back to the current question/task when your mind wanders or anxiety spikes.
- Use lunch breaks and the evening between exam days for **complete mental reset and recovery** – absolutely NO debriefing questions or last-minute studying.
- Focus on executing your practiced strategies and managing your responses to challenges, accepting that perfection is impossible and competence under pressure is the goal.
- Acknowledge completing the exam as a major accomplishment and prioritize rest and recovery immediately afterward.[21]

Part 4: Practice Questions

Practice Exam 1

Below is a 100-question multiple-choice mock bar exam covering the seven core MBE subjects. Each question is followed by the correct answer and a brief explanation.

Civil Procedure (14 Questions)

1. Under the Federal Rules of Civil Procedure, a defendant must serve an answer within how many days of being served the summons and complaint?

- A) 14 days
- B) 21 days
- C) 28 days
- D) 30 days
  Answer: B
  Explanation: Rule 12(a)(1)(A)(i) sets a 21-day period for an answer.

2. A federal court's power to hear state-law claims related to a federal question is called

- A) Original jurisdiction
- B) Supplemental jurisdiction
- C) Removal jurisdiction
- D) Venue jurisdiction
  Answer: B
  Explanation: Supplemental jurisdiction under 28 U.S.C. §1367 covers state claims linked to federal ones.

3. Under the Erie doctrine, a federal court in a diversity case must apply

- A) Federal substantive law
- B) State substantive law
- C) Federal procedure

- D) Federal common law
  Answer: B
  Explanation: Erie v. Tompkins requires state substantive law in diversity suits.

4. Which FRCP motion is available to challenge failure to state a claim upon which relief can be granted?

- A) 12(b)(1)
- B) 12(b)(2)
- C) 12(b)(3)
- D) 12(b)(6)
  Answer: D
  Explanation: Rule 12(b)(6) permits dismissal for failure to state a claim.

5. Forum non conveniens allows a court to

- A) Transfer venue to another federal district
- B) Dismiss a case when an alternate forum is more suitable
- C) Remove case to state court
- D) Consolidate actions in different districts
  Answer: B
  Explanation: It permits dismissal if another forum is substantially more appropriate.

6. Under Rule 26, initial disclosures must include all of the following except

- A) Documents that support claims
- B) Computation of damages
- C) Copies of insurance agreements
- D) Witness statements prepared for litigation
  Answer: D
  Explanation: Rule 26(a)(1) excludes witness statements prepared for trial.

7. Claim preclusion bars a subsequent suit when

- A) Claims arise from different transactions
- B) First suit ended in judgment on the merits
- C) Parties are different
- D) Court lacks jurisdiction
  Answer: B
  Explanation: A final merits judgment prevents re-litigation of the same claim.

8. Issue preclusion prevents re-litigation of issues that were

- A) Relevant to a different claim
- B) Actually litigated and essential to prior judgment
- C) Agreed by parties afterward
- D) Raised in a later suit
  Answer: B
  Explanation: Only issues necessary to the first judgment are barred.

9. A motion to remand for lack of subject-matter jurisdiction must be made

- A) At any time before trial
- B) Within 30 days of removal notice
- C) Before removal only
- D) Within 14 days of filing
  Answer: B
  Explanation: The remand motion is due within 30 days of the notice of removal.

10. Diversity jurisdiction requires complete diversity and

- A) Case value over $50,000
- B) Case value over $75,000
- C) Case value over $100,000

- D) Federal question
  Answer: B
  Explanation: 28 U.S.C. §1332 sets the amount in controversy above $75,000.

11. General personal jurisdiction exists when a defendant's contacts with the forum state are

- A) Isolated and accidental
- B) Continuous and systematic
- C) Merely related to a single act
- D) Nonexistent
  Answer: B
  Explanation: Continuous, systematic contacts support general jurisdiction.

12. Specific personal jurisdiction requires that the plaintiff's claim

- A) Arise from defendant's forum contacts
- B) Be based on state law only
- C) Involve property in the forum
- D) Involve federal law
  Answer: A
  Explanation: The claim must relate to the defendant's activities in the forum.

13. Which element is not required for class certification under Rule 23?

- A) Numerosity
- B) Commonality
- C) Typicality
- D) Mandatory mediation
  Answer: D
  Explanation: Numerosity, commonality, typicality and adequacy are required.

14. Rule 42(a) of the FRCP allows a court to

- A) Consolidate actions involving common questions

- B) Dismiss for failure to state a claim
- C) Transfer a case to a different district
- D) Remand to state court
  Answer: A
  Explanation: Rule 42(a) permits consolidation of cases with common legal or factual issues.

Constitutional Law (14 Questions)

15. Under strict scrutiny, a law restricting speech must be

- A) Narrowly tailored to serve a compelling state interest
- B) Loosely applied to all speech
- C) Based on marketplace of ideas
- D) Approved by Congress
  Answer: A
  Explanation: Strict scrutiny demands narrow tailoring to a compelling interest.

16. Commercial speech restrictions require

- A) Advancement of a substantial government interest
- B) Strict necessity
- C) Prior restraint
- D) Content neutrality
  Answer: A
  Explanation: Under Central Hudson, regulation must directly advance a substantial interest.

17. The Lemon test for the Establishment Clause includes all except

- A) Secular purpose
- B) Primary effect must not advance religion
- C) No excessive government entanglement

- D) Complete prohibition of religious symbols
  Answer: D
  Explanation: Lemon v. Kurtzman covers purpose, effect and entanglement prongs.

18. A law classifying on the basis of gender is subject to

- A) Intermediate scrutiny
- B) Strict scrutiny
- C) Rational basis
- D) No scrutiny
  Answer: A
  Explanation: Gender is a quasi-suspect classification requiring intermediate review.

19. Procedural due process guarantees

- A) Notice and opportunity to be heard before deprivation
- B) Jury trial in all civil cases
- C) Free exercise of religion
- D) Equal protection
  Answer: A
  Explanation: Both notice and an opportunity to be heard are required before depriving life, liberty or property.

20. Substantive due process protects

- A) Fundamental rights from undue government interference
- B) All economic legislation
- C) Jury selection procedures
- D) Boundary disputes
  Answer: A
  Explanation: It guards rights such as privacy against arbitrary laws.

21. Congress's power to regulate trade among states is found in

- A) Commerce Clause
- B) Taxing Clause
- C) Property Clause
- D) Due Process Clause
  Answer: A
  Explanation: Article I, Section 8, Clause 3 grants this power.

22. The Supremacy Clause declares

- A) Federal law overrides conflicting state statutes
- B) State law always takes precedence
- C) States share power evenly
- D) Treaties are subordinate to state law
  Answer: A
  Explanation: Article VI makes federal law supreme over state laws.

23. Under the Dormant Commerce Clause, discriminatory state laws must show

- A) No reasonable nondiscriminatory alternatives
- B) Only rational basis
- C) Congressional approval
- D) Compliance with state due process
  Answer: A
  Explanation: Discriminatory laws must be narrowly tailored with no alternatives.

24. Executive orders derive authority from

- A) Constitutional powers and statutes
- B) State legislatures
- C) International treaties
- D) Judicial precedent
  Answer: A

Explanation: They rest on executive branch powers and congressional delegation.

25. Judicial review was established in

- A) Marbury v. Madison
- B) McCulloch v. Maryland
- C) Dred Scott v. Sandford
- D) Plessy v. Ferguson
  Answer: A
  Explanation: Marbury v. Madison created the doctrine of judicial review.

26. The Privileges and Immunities Clause prevents states from

- A) Discriminating against out-of-state citizens in fundamental rights
- B) Enforcing due process
- C) Regulating commerce
- D) Taxing goods
  Answer: A
  Explanation: Article IV bars discrimination against nonresidents regarding basic rights.

27. A state law requiring marriage as a condition for professional licensure is

- A) Invalid under Privileges and Immunities
- B) Valid exercise of police power
- C) Immune from challenge
- D) Enforced by Supremacy Clause
  Answer: A
  Explanation: It unfairly discriminates against out-of-state applicants.

28. School-sponsored prayer in a public school violates the

- A) Establishment Clause
- B) Free Speech Clause

- C) Equal Protection Clause
- D) Due Process Clause
  Answer: A
  Explanation: Official endorsement of prayer breaches separation of church and state.

Contracts (15 Questions)

29. A valid offer requires

- A) Intent to be bound, definite terms, and communication
- B) Invitation to negotiate
- C) Advertisement only
- D) Silence
  Answer: A
  Explanation: An offer must show commitment, clarity and be communicated to the offeree.

30. Under common law, an acceptance that adds new terms acts as

- A) Counteroffer
- B) Acceptance
- C) Revocation
- D) Lapse of offer
  Answer: A
  Explanation: The mirror-image rule requires acceptance to match the offer exactly.

31. Past consideration is

- A) Insufficient to support a contract
- B) Always binding
- C) A gift

- D) A novation
  Answer: A
  Explanation: Only present or future consideration counts.

32. Promissory estoppel may enforce a promise if

- A) Promisee reasonably relies to avoid injustice
- B) Offer is revoked
- C) Contract is fully executed
- D) Promise is gratuitous
  Answer: A
  Explanation: Courts enforce reliance-based promises to prevent unfair results.

33. The Statute of Frauds does not require a writing for

- A) Contracts performable within one year
- B) Sale of goods over $500
- C) Real estate transfers
- D) Surety agreements
  Answer: A
  Explanation: Only contracts that cannot be performed within one year must be in writing.

34. The parol evidence rule excludes prior agreements that

- A) Contradict a fully integrated contract
- B) Clarify ambiguous terms
- C) Demonstrate fraud
- D) Show course of dealing
  Answer: A
  Explanation: Fully integrated writings cannot be contradicted by earlier agreements.

35. Under UCC, an acceptance with additional terms between merchants is

- A) Part of contract unless they materially alter it
- B) Always a rejection
- C) Void
- D) Automatically binding
  Answer: A
  Explanation: UCC §2-207 adds terms unless they materially change the deal.

36. UCC statute of limitations for sale of goods is

- A) Four years
- B) Three years
- C) Two years
- D) Five years
  Answer: A
  Explanation: Section 2-725 prescribes a four-year period.

37. In a UCC shipment contract, risk of loss passes when

- A) Goods are delivered to carrier
- B) Goods reach buyer
- C) Title transfers
- D) Contract forms
  Answer: A
  Explanation: Shipment contracts shift risk upon delivery to the carrier.

38. Substantial performance allows a party to recover

- A) Contract price minus damages for defects
- B) No payment
- C) Full liquidated damages
- D) Specific performance only
  Answer: A
  Explanation: Minor deviations lead to deductions, not denial of recovery.

39. Impracticability discharges duties when performance becomes

- A) Unduly burdensome due to unforeseen circumstances
- B) More expensive by 10%
- C) Impossible to negotiate
- D) Dispreferred by one party
  Answer: A
  Explanation: Both common law and UCC excuse performance for extreme hardship.

40. A third-party intended beneficiary may

- A) Enforce a contract when it was meant for their benefit
- B) Sue only as an incidental beneficiary
- C) Assign rights only
- D) Be bound only if signing
  Answer: A
  Explanation: Intended beneficiaries gain enforcement rights.

41. Assignment of rights is invalid if it

- A) Materially increases obligor's burden
- B) Benefits all parties equally
- C) Is gratuitous
- D) Occurs after performance
  Answer: A
  Explanation: Assignments cannot alter the obligor's duties.

42. Delegation of duties cannot occur when contract involves

- A) Unique personal services
- B) Sale of goods
- C) Real estate

- D) Agency relationships
  Answer: A
  Explanation: Personal service contracts requiring special skill are non-delegable.

43. Expectation damages aim to

- A) Place the injured party in the position they would have been in if performance occurred
- B) Restore them to the original position
- C) Punish the breaching party
- D) Award nominal sum
  Answer: A
  Explanation: They cover the benefits lost due to breach.

Criminal Law & Procedure (14 Questions)

44. Actus reus refers to

- A) Physical act or omission
- B) Guilty mind
- C) Intoxication
- D) Insanity
  Answer: A
  Explanation: It demands a voluntary act or failure when there is a duty.

45. Specific intent requires

- A) Intent to bring about a prohibited result
- B) Knowledge of legality
- C) Recklessness
- D) Strict liability
  Answer: A
  Explanation: It involves a conscious aim toward a particular outcome.

46. A strict liability crime imposes

- A) No mental-state requirement
- B) Proof of negligence
- C) Requirement of intent
- D) Legal impossibility
  Answer: A
  Explanation: The act alone suffices for guilt, regardless of intent.

47. First-degree murder typically requires

- A) Premeditation and deliberation
- B) Heat of passion
- C) Felony murder only
- D) Accident
  Answer: A
  Explanation: It involves a planned, intentional killing.

48. A valid search warrant needs

- A) Probable cause supported by oath
- B) Reasonable suspicion
- C) Consent
- D) Mere speculation
  Answer: A
  Explanation: Warrants must rest on sworn statements showing probable cause.

49. The exclusionary rule bars introduction of

- A) Evidence obtained in violation of the Fourth Amendment
- B) All hearsay
- C) Expert testimony

- D) Prior convictions
  Answer: A
  Explanation: Illegally seized evidence is inadmissible.

50. Miranda warnings protect the right against

- A) Self-incrimination
- B) Cruel punishment
- C) Unreasonable fines
- D) Speedy trial
  Answer: A
  Explanation: They inform suspects of Fifth Amendment rights in custody.

51. Under the Sixth Amendment, the right to counsel attaches at

- A) Initiation of adversary judicial proceedings
- B) Police interview only
- C) Detention for questioning
- D) Appeal
  Answer: A
  Explanation: It applies after charges, arraignment or indictment.

52. Double jeopardy prohibits

- A) Multiple prosecutions for the same offense after acquittal
- B) Collateral civil suits
- C) Sentencing enhancements
- D) New trials upon retrial
  Answer: A
  Explanation: It bars retrial after acquittal or conviction for the same crime.

53. The test for speedy-trial claims involves

- A) Balancing private and public interests
- B) Fixed 60-day deadline

- C) Strict timeframe for all crimes
- D) Automatic dismissal if indicted late
  Answer: A
  Explanation: Barker v. Wingo balances length of delay, reasons, and prejudice.

54. Confrontation Clause guarantees

- A) Right to cross-examine adverse witnesses
- B) Right to hearsay testimony
- C) Right to privacy
- D) Right to information in civil cases
  Answer: A
  Explanation: It secures cross-examination at trial.

55. A custodial interrogation requires

- A) Miranda warnings
- B) Search warrant
- C) Grand jury return
- D) Bail hearing
  Answer: A
  Explanation: Warnings apply when a suspect's freedom is restrained.

56. Insanity defense under M'Naghten tests whether

- A) Defendant knew wrongfulness of act
- B) Defendant was intoxicated
- C) Jury was biased
- D) Evidence was stolen
  Answer: A
  Explanation: It focuses on cognitive capacity to distinguish right from wrong.

Evidence (15 Questions)

58. Evidence is relevant if it

- A) Makes a fact more or less probable
- B) Is prejudicial only
- C) Is inadmissible hearsay
- D) Has no probative value
  Answer: A
  Explanation: Relevance requires tendency to affect probability of a material fact.

59. The rule against hearsay excludes statements

- A) Made outside court offered to prove truth
- B) By party-opponents
- C) Animations
- D) Machine records
  Answer: A
  Explanation: Hearsay is an out-of-court statement used for its truth.

60. Present sense impressions are admissible if the statement describes an event

- A) While perceiving it or immediately after
- B) Under oath
- C) Days later
- D) In a diary
  Answer: A
  Explanation: Contemporaneous description reduces risk of fabrication.

61. Excited utterances are statements made

- A) Under stress of a startling event
- B) In calm reflection
- C) In writing

- D) After consulting counsel
  Answer: A
  Explanation: Stress of excitement provides sufficient reliability.

62. Business-records exception applies to records made

- A) In regular course of business near time of event
- B) During litigation only
- C) By casual observers
- D) In public hearings
  Answer: A
  Explanation: Routine business entries are presumed trustworthy.

63. A party-opponent's statement is treated as

- A) Not hearsay
- B) Inadmissible
- C) Privileged
- D) Judicial notice
  Answer: A
  Explanation: Admissions by a party are excluded from the hearsay rule.

64. Best-evidence rule requires

- A) Original writing to prove contents
- B) Secondary evidence always
- C) Copy preference
- D) Oral summary
  Answer: A
  Explanation: Originals are necessary to prove the content of a writing.

65. Lay-witness opinion is allowed when based on

- A) Perception and helpfulness to fact-finder
- B) Expert qualification

- C) Unsupported belief
- D) Scientific method
  Answer: A
  Explanation: Lay opinions must stem from direct observation.

66. Daubert standard guides admissibility of

- A) Expert testimony
- B) Hearsay evidence
- C) Blueprint plans
- D) Prior convictions
  Answer: A
  Explanation: Courts assess the reliability and relevance of expert methods.

67. Attorney-client privilege protects

- A) Confidential legal communications
- B) Public statements
- C) Business strategies
- D) Admissions in open court
  Answer: A
  Explanation: It shields private communications made for legal advice.

68. Spousal testimony privilege can be asserted by

- A) Witness spouse in adverse trial
- B) Any party in civil case
- C) Employer
- D) Grand juror
  Answer: A
  Explanation: It bars compulsion of testimony by the spouse of the accused.

69. Character evidence to show propensity in a criminal case is

- A) Generally inadmissible

- B) Always admissible
- C) Permitted for motive only
- D) Required by rule
  Answer: A
  Explanation: Rules ban character evidence to prove conduct in conformity.

70. Prior inconsistent statements may be used to

- A) Impeach witness credibility
- B) Prove truth of the matter asserted
- C) Replace direct evidence
- D) Satisfy personal jurisdiction
  Answer: A
  Explanation: They serve to show contradictions in testimony.

71. Subsequent remedial measures are inadmissible to prove

- A) Liability
- B) Ownership
- C) Defect
- D) Witness bias
  Answer: A
  Explanation: They cannot be used to show negligence or fault.

72. Offers to pay medical expenses are admissible to prove

- A) Payment of expenses only
- B) Admission of liability
- C) Negligence per se
- D) Property ownership
  Answer: A
  Explanation: Payment offers are allowed without inferring liability.

Real Property (14 Questions)

73. Fee simple absolute is

- A) Largest estate without conditions
- B) Life estate
- C) Leasehold
- D) Future interest
  Answer: A
  Explanation: It grants full ownership indefinitely.

74. Fee simple determinable ends automatically upon

- A) Occurrence of a specified event
- B) Death of current owner
- C) Conveyance to a third party
- D) Expiration of lease
  Answer: A
  Explanation: FSD terminates when the stated condition occurs.

75. Joint tenancy includes

- A) Right of survivorship
- B) Transferability only
- C) Remainder interest
- D) Lease for years
  Answer: A
  Explanation: JT requires survivorship plus unities of time and title.

76. Tenancy in common grants

- A) Individual shares without survivorship
- B) Whole unit ownership by all
- C) Life estate

- D) Leasehold interest
  Answer: A
  Explanation: Each tenant holds a distinct, transferable share.

77. An easement appurtenant benefits

- A) Dominant estate
- B) Servient estate
- C) Public at large
- D) Licensee
  Answer: A
  Explanation: It runs with the land to serve an adjoining property owner.

78. An easement by necessity arises when

- A) Landlocked parcel requires access
- B) Neighbor grants permission
- C) Express grant is omitted
- D) License is revoked
  Answer: A
  Explanation: Necessity easements form when no other access exists.

79. Adverse possession requires

- A) Actual, open, notorious, exclusive, hostile, continuous possession
- B) Written permission
- C) License status
- D) Quiet-title suit
  Answer: A
  Explanation: All elements must exist for the statutory period.

80. Equitable conversion shifts risk of loss to buyer upon

- A) Contract signing
- B) Closing

- C) Recording the deed
- D) Delivery of the deed
  Answer: A
  Explanation: Buyer holds equitable title after contract formation.

81. Under notice recording acts, a subsequent purchaser prevails if

- A) They purchased without notice of prior interest
- B) They record later
- C) They knew of the prior claim
- D) They file a lis pendens
  Answer: A
  Explanation: A bona fide purchaser without notice prevails under notice statutes.

82. A variance permits

- A) Deviation from zoning rules for hardship
- B) Rezoning an entire district
- C) Permanent bypass of building code
- D) Creating easements
  Answer: A
  Explanation: It grants relief for practical difficulties.

83. A restrictive covenant runs with the land if it meets requirements of

- A) Intent, touch and concern, privity, and notice
- B) Equal protection
- C) Recording only
- D) Judicial hearing
  Answer: A
  Explanation: These four conditions bind successors.

84. A fixture is

- A) Personal property permanently attached to land
- B) Leasehold interest
- C) Chattel always removable
- D) Security interest
  Answer: A
  Explanation: Attachments intended as permanent additions become part of real estate.

85. Assignment of a lease transfers

- A) Entire remaining interest under the lease
- B) Sublease rights only
- C) Reversion interest
- D) Mortgage rights
  Answer: A
  Explanation: Assignee holds the leasehold estate and privity of estate.

86. The right of redemption allows a mortgagor to regain title by

- A) Paying the debt before foreclosure sale
- B) After the sale
- C) Without payment
- D) Only with court order
  Answer: A
  Explanation: The equitable right ends at the sale; payment before sale restores title.

Torts (14 Questions)

87. Battery requires

- A) Intentional harmful or offensive contact
- B) Apprehension only
- C) Property harm

- D) Words alone
  Answer: A
  Explanation: Unwanted contact with another's person is sufficient.

88. False imprisonment is

- A) Intentional confinement of another without consent
- B) Publication of false statement
- C) Trespass to chattels
- D) Strict liability tort
  Answer: A
  Explanation: Confinement within fixed boundaries against one's will.

89. Intentional infliction of emotional distress requires

- A) Outrageous conduct causing severe distress
- B) Minor discomfort
- C) Property damage
- D) Consent
  Answer: A
  Explanation: Conduct must exceed limits tolerated by society.

90. Trespass to land requires

- A) Intentional entry onto someone else's property
- B) Injury to the land
- C) Borrowing without permission
- D) Strict liability
  Answer: A
  Explanation: Intentional invasion is enough, even without harm.

91. In negligence, duty refers to

- A) Legal obligation to conform to a standard of care
- B) Breach of contract

- C) Causation
- D) Damages
  Answer: A
  Explanation: It defines what an actor must do to avoid liability.

92. Breach occurs when

- A) Conduct falls below the standard of a reasonable person
- B) Harm occurs
- C) Intent is shown
- D) Strict liability applies
  Answer: A
  Explanation: Failure to meet care expectations constitutes breach.

93. Proximate cause limits liability to harms that

- A) Are foreseeable results of the act
- B) Occur decades later
- C) Are remote consequences
- D) Arise after a bargain
  Answer: A
  Explanation: Liability requires a reasonably predictable link.

94. Comparative negligence reduces recovery by

- A) Plaintiff's percentage of fault
- B) Preventing any recovery
- C) Awarding punitive damages
- D) Doubling defendant's burden
  Answer: A
  Explanation: Damages are decreased by the plaintiff's share of fault.

95. Strict liability for abnormally dangerous activities applies to

- A) High-risk activities even if precautions are taken

- B) Ordinary negligence
- C) Property disputes
- D) Trespass
  Answer: A
  Explanation: Unusual activities posing severe harm trigger liability.

96. Under the risk-utility test for design defects, plaintiff must show

- A) A safer, feasible alternative design existed
- B) Manufacturer was negligent only
- C) Buyer misuse
- D) Express warranty
  Answer: A
  Explanation: Courts weigh risks, costs and available alternatives.

97. Manufacturing defect strict liability applies if a product

- A) Deviates from intended design causing danger
- B) Is misused
- C) Meets specifications
- D) Is modified after sale
  Answer: A
  Explanation: Production flaws make a product unreasonably dangerous.

98. For defamation, a statement must be

- A) False and published to a third party
- B) True only
- C) Pure opinion
- D) Privileged
  Answer: A
  Explanation: Publication of a false, defamatory statement injures reputation.

99. A qualified privilege in defamation is lost if

- A) Statement is made with malice
- B) It is true
- C) It is honestly believed
- D) A correction is offered
  Answer: A
  Explanation: Malice defeats the protection of privilege.

100. Public nuisance involves

- A) Unreasonable interference with rights common to the public
- B) Private property damage only
- C) Defamation
- D) Contract breach
  Answer: A
  Explanation: It affects the community at large rather than an individual.

Practice Exam 2

Civil Procedure (14 Questions)

1. Under FRCP Rule 15(a), a party may amend its pleading once as a matter of course within how many days after serving it?

- A) 14 days
- B) 21 days
- C) 28 days
- D) 30 days
  Answer: A
  Explanation: Rule 15(a)(1) permits one free amendment within 14 days of service.

2. Which Federal Rule governs summary judgment?

- A) Rule 30
- B) Rule 50
- C) Rule 56
- D) Rule 65
  Answer: C
  Explanation: Rule 56 sets requirements for summary judgment motions.

3. To effect service of process, a defendant must sign a waiver under Rule 4 only if served by

- A) Mail with return receipt
- B) Personal delivery
- C) Judicial officer
- D) Publication
  Answer: A
  Explanation: Rule 4(d) allows service by mail with a waiver request.

4. For diversity jurisdiction, a corporation is a citizen of

- A) State of incorporation only
- B) State of principal place of business only
- C) Both state of incorporation and principal place of business
- D) Any state where it conducts business
  Answer: C
  Explanation: Corporations are citizens of both their incorporation and principal place of business.

5. A forum-selection clause in a contract is generally

- A) Unenforceable under public policy
- B) Given substantial weight by courts
- C) Treated as per se unreasonable
- D) Voidable only by the defendant
  Answer: B
  Explanation: Courts uphold such clauses absent strong countervailing reasons.

6. The outcome-determination test under Erie asks whether applying federal procedure would

- A) Affect outcome significantly in litigation
- B) Be favored by federal courts
- C) Be cheaper for the parties
- D) Align with international norms
  Answer: A
  Explanation: If choice of law affects the outcome, state substantive law applies.

7. To transfer venue under 28 U.S.C. §1404(a), the movant must show

- A) Original venue was improper
- B) Convenience of parties and witnesses and interest of justice

- C) No personal jurisdiction
- D) Lack of a federal issue
  Answer: B
  Explanation: Section 1404(a) balances convenience and justice factors.

8. A Rule 12(e) motion asks the court to

- A) Dismiss for insufficient service
- B) Strike redundant matter
- C) Order a more definite statement
- D) Stay proceedings
  Answer: C
  Explanation: Rule 12(e) seeks clarification when a pleading is vague or ambiguous.

9. Under Rule 26(b)(1), discovery scope includes information that is

- A) Irrelevant but harmless
- B) Nonprivileged and reasonably calculated to lead to admissible evidence
- C) Privileged if waived
- D) Only available before trial
  Answer: B
  Explanation: Discovery allows relevant evidence leading to admissible proof.

10. An interlocutory appeal under 28 U.S.C. §1292(b) requires the district court to certify that

- A) A final judgment will follow
- B) The order involves a controlling question of law with substantial ground for difference of opinion
- C) The parties consent
- D) The appellate court invited it
  Answer: B

Explanation: Certification enables appeal of non-final orders in exceptional cases.

11. Under Rule 23(b)(3), damages class certification requires that common issues

- A) Predominate over individual ones and that a class action is the superior method
- B) Affect each member identically
- C) Be manageable by the judge alone
- D) Exclude complex issues
  Answer: A
  Explanation: Predominance and superiority guide class-wide damage actions.

12. Rule 60(b)(6) provides relief for

- A) Clerical errors only
- B) Any reason that justifies relief when no specific ground applies
- C) Lack of jurisdiction
- D) Settlement agreements
  Answer: B
  Explanation: Clause (6) covers any extraordinary circumstance.

13. A party seeking to vacate a default judgment under Rule 60(b)(1) must act

- A) Within one year
- B) Within a reasonable time
- C) After six months
- D) Before trial
  Answer: B
  Explanation: "Reasonable time" depends on the circumstances.

14. A federal court may certify a question to a state supreme court when

- A) There is no controlling state law
- B) The case is on appeal

- C) Venue is contested
- D) Jurisdiction is disputed
  Answer: A
  Explanation: Certification seeks authoritative state law interpretation.

Constitutional Law (14 Questions)

15. Under the First Amendment, a law punishing symbolic speech is subject to

- A) Rational basis
- B) Intermediate scrutiny
- C) Strict scrutiny
- D) No scrutiny
  Answer: C
  Explanation: Symbolic speech restrictions must serve a compelling interest narrowly.

16. A gender-based classification in government benefits is evaluated under

- A) Rational basis
- B) Intermediate scrutiny
- C) Strict scrutiny
- D) No scrutiny
  Answer: B
  Explanation: Gender classifications require an important government objective.

17. State endorsement of religious teachings in public schools violates the

- A) Free Exercise Clause
- B) Establishment Clause
- C) Equal Protection Clause

- D) Free Speech Clause
  Answer: B
  Explanation: State-sponsored religion breaches the Establishment Clause.

18. Age-based classifications typically receive

- A) Strict scrutiny
- B) Intermediate scrutiny
- C) Rational basis review
- D) No constitutional review
  Answer: C
  Explanation: Age is not a suspect or quasi-suspect class, so rational basis applies.

19. Congress's power to impose taxes lies in the

- A) Commerce Clause
- B) Taxing and Spending Clause
- C) Contract Clause
- D) Necessary and Proper Clause
  Answer: B
  Explanation: Article I grants taxing authority for the general welfare.

20. The Takings Clause requires the government to provide just compensation if

- A) Property is regulated
- B) Physical property is permanently appropriated
- C) Taxes exceed 1%
- D) Zoning changes occur
  Answer: B
  Explanation: Physical appropriation constitutes a taking requiring compensation.

21. The president's treaty power requires

- A) House approval
- B) Two-thirds Senate ratification
- C) Supreme Court consent
- D) Bicameralism
  Answer: B
  Explanation: Treaties need a two-thirds Senate vote.

22. A later federal statute conflicting with a treaty is

- A) Invalid
- B) Prevailing if enacted later
- C) Subject to judicial nullification
- D) Always subordinate
  Answer: B
  Explanation: Later statutes supersede prior treaties if clearly intended.

23. The 14th Amendment's Privileges or Immunities Clause protects

- A) All privileges of U.S. citizenship from state interference
- B) None beyond Due Process protections
- C) State citizenship rights only
- D) Foreign nationals
  Answer: A
  Explanation: It secures fundamental rights from state abridgment.

24. The doctrine that courts avoid constitutional rulings when possible is

- A) Judicial restraint
- B) Constitutional avoidance
- C) Stare decisis
- D) Sovereign immunity
  Answer: B
  Explanation: Courts interpret statutes to avert constitutional questions.

25. A prior restraint on publication is

- A) Presumptively invalid
- B) Valid if content-neutral
- C) Reviewed under rational basis
- D) Favored to protect privacy
  Answer: A
  Explanation: Censorship before publication is broadly disfavored.

26. The Speech or Debate Clause provides immunity for

- A) Lobbying activities
- B) Legislative acts within the official sphere
- C) Fundraising speeches
- D) Truthful statements outside Congress
  Answer: B
  Explanation: It shields lawmakers for legislative acts.

27. Under substantive due process, a law infringing a fundamental right must be

- A) Rationally related to a legitimate purpose
- B) Narrowly tailored to a compelling interest
- C) Broadly applied
- D) Approved by the courts
  Answer: B
  Explanation: Fundamental rights demand strict scrutiny.

28. Channels of interstate commerce include

- A) Persons crossing state lines
- B) Intrastate manufacturing only
- C) State government employees

- D) Local city streets
  Answer: A
  Explanation: Transportation of persons and goods across state lines falls under the Commerce Clause.

Contracts (15 Questions)

29. An offer terminates by lapse when

- A) The offeree fails to accept within a reasonable time or the time stated
- B) Offeror changes mind immediately
- C) Offeree rejects then reaccepts
- D) Offer made to multiple offerees
  Answer: A
  Explanation: Offers expire after the specified or reasonable period.

30. A requirements contract under the UCC obliges the buyer to purchase

- A) All needed goods exclusively from the seller
- B) A minimum quantity only
- C) Unlimited goods anywhere
- D) Non-conforming goods only
  Answer: A
  Explanation: The buyer agrees to buy all its requirements exclusively from that seller.

31. Under UCC, a merchant's firm offer in writing remains open without consideration for

- A) Up to three months
- B) Six months
- C) One month

- D) An indefinite period
  Answer: A
  Explanation: UCC §2-205 fixes a maximum of three months.

32. Acceptance by performance creates a contract when

- A) The offer invites such performance and the offeree begins performance
- B) Offeror expects payment
- C) Offeree mails acceptance only
- D) Performance is minor
  Answer: A
  Explanation: Unilateral offers form contracts when performance begins or is completed.

33. Between non-merchants, under UCC battle of forms, additional terms

- A) Are proposals that must be separately accepted
- B) Automatically add to the contract
- C) Void the entire contract
- D) Create a new offer by the merchant
  Answer: A
  Explanation: Terms are mere proposals needing express acceptance.

34. An accord and satisfaction discharges the original duty when

- A) The new agreement is executed in satisfaction of the prior obligation
- B) A party refuses to perform
- C) A suit is filed
- D) The statute of limitations expires
  Answer: A
  Explanation: Performance of the accord releases the original contract claim.

35. Modification of a sale-of-goods contract under UCC requires

- A) A good-faith agreement; no new consideration is needed

- B) A written modification only
- C) Court authorization
- D) Unanimous merchant approval only
Answer: A
Explanation: UCC permits modifications by agreement made in good faith.

36. Under the Statute of Frauds, a guarantee agreement must

- A) Be in writing signed by the guarantor
- B) Be in writing signed by the obligee
- C) Be oral if witnessed
- D) Include a price term
Answer: A
Explanation: Suretyship contracts require the guarantor's signature.

37. Common-law duress voids a contract when voluntary consent is lacking due to

- A) A wrongful threat leaving no reasonable alternative
- B) Hard bargaining
- C) Minor frustration
- D) Superior knowledge
Answer: A
Explanation: Coercive threats that overbear the will vitiate consent.

38. Economic duress occurs when one party's wrongful threats

- A) Leave the other no reasonable choice but to agree
- B) Increase price slightly
- C) Apply only in labor contracts
- D) Are morally blameworthy but lawful
Answer: A
Explanation: Coercion by economic pressure can render a contract voidable.

39. A court may refuse to enforce an unconscionable contract clause when

- A) It finds the terms so unfair they shock the conscience
- B) Both parties are merchants
- C) The contract is in writing
- D) Performance has begun
  Answer: A
  Explanation: Unconscionability permits courts to sever or refuse oppressive terms.

40. An arbitration clause in a contract is generally

- A) Enforceable unless unconscionable or violates public policy
- B) Per se unenforceable
- C) Only valid in federal question cases
- D) Always void in consumer contracts
  Answer: A
  Explanation: The FAA favors arbitration absent strong contrary reasons.

41. A condition precedent in a contract must occur

- A) Before the contractual duty arises
- B) After all duties are performed
- C) Simultaneously with payment
- D) Never
  Answer: A
  Explanation: A condition precedent triggers an obligation upon fulfillment.

42. A novation differs from an assignment by

- A) Replacing one party with a new one, extinguishing original obligations
- B) Transferring benefits only
- C) Requiring court approval
- D) Creating third-party beneficiaries
  Answer: A

Explanation: Novation substitutes a party and extinguishes the original contract.

43. Common-law impossibility discharges obligations when performance becomes

- A) Truly impossible, not merely burdensome or costly
- B) Uneconomical
- C) Inconvenient
- D) Unprofitable
  Answer: A
  Explanation: Only objective impossibility excuses duty.

44. A liquidated damages clause is enforceable when

- A) Damages are difficult to estimate and the amount is a reasonable forecast
- B) It is punitive by nature
- C) It fixes a large penalty
- D) It is unconditional
  Answer: A
  Explanation: Such clauses must reflect a genuine pre-estimate, not a penalty.

45. Specific performance is available for

- A) Unique items or real estate when money damages are inadequate
- B) All breach of contract cases
- C) Personal service agreements
- D) Employment contracts
  Answer: A
  Explanation: An equitable remedy for unique subject matter.

Criminal Law & Procedure (14 Questions)

46. A negligence standard for mens rea requires proof that the defendant

- A) Should have been aware of a substantial risk
- B) Intended the harm
- C) Acted recklessly knowingly
- D) Had no mental fault
  Answer: A
  Explanation: Criminal negligence is failure to perceive a substantial risk.

47. The felony-murder rule imposes liability if death occurs during the commission or attempt of

- A) Dangerous felonies
- B) Petty theft
- C) Traffic offenses only
- D) Regulatory violations
  Answer: A
  Explanation: BARRK felonies include burglary, arson, robbery, rape, kidnapping.

48. Conspiracy requires agreement plus

- A) An overt act by one conspirator in furtherance
- B) Commission of the substantive offense always
- C) Unilateral intent
- D) A confidential relationship
  Answer: A
  Explanation: Modern law demands any overt act toward the conspiracy.

49. Withdrawal from conspiracy may be achieved by

- A) Communicating intent to withdraw and thwarting objectives
- B) Failing to attend a meeting
- C) Passive non-participation

- D) Police interview
  Answer: A
  Explanation: An affirmative act to defeat the conspiracy relieves liability for future crimes.

50. The defense of diminished capacity addresses

- A) Lack of specific intent due to mental defect
- B) Insanity under M'Naghten
- C) Voluntary intoxication only
- D) Strict liability offenses
  Answer: A
  Explanation: It negates the specific mental state required for certain crimes.

51. A search incident to arrest must be conducted

- A) Contemporaneously to a lawful arrest and within the immediate control area
- B) Within 24 hours
- C) Anywhere police suspect evidence
- D) Without probable cause
  Answer: A
  Explanation: Scope is limited to the arrestee's person and nearby reach.

52. A stop and frisk under Terry v. Ohio requires

- A) Reasonable suspicion of criminal activity and belief the suspect is armed
- B) Probable cause
- C) An arrest warrant
- D) Consent
  Answer: A
  Explanation: Limited search justified by officer safety and specific suspicion.

53. A grand jury indictment is required for

- A) Federal felony prosecution
- B) Misdemeanor petty offenses
- C) Civil contempt
- D) Traffic infractions
  Answer: A
  Explanation: The Fifth Amendment demands a grand jury for serious federal crimes.

54. Double jeopardy does not bar prosecution for the same act under distinct statutes if

- A) Congress clearly authorizes cumulative punishments
- B) Charges arise from identical elements
- C) The sentence is served
- D) There is a warrantless arrest
  Answer: A
  Explanation: Blockburger test applies unless legislative intent allows cumulative punishment.

55. The Confrontation Clause applies to

- A) Testimonial statements by non-testifying witnesses
- B) All hearsay exceptions
- C) Civil trials only
- D) Grand jury proceedings
  Answer: A
  Explanation: Testimonial out-of-court statements require cross-examination opportunity.

56. Miranda warnings may be waived if

- A) The waiver is knowing, voluntary, and intelligent
- B) The suspect is indigent

- C) The case involves national security
- D) Warnings are given after conviction
  Answer: A
  Explanation: A valid waiver ensures suspect understands rights.

57. The remedy for a Fourth Amendment violation is

- A) Exclusionary rule barring illegally obtained evidence
- B) Civil contempt
- C) Dismissal of all charges
- D) Automatic damages
  Answer: A
  Explanation: Illegally seized evidence cannot be used in prosecution.

Evidence (15 Questions)

58. A fact may be judicially noticed if it is

- A) Not subject to reasonable dispute because it is generally known or capable of accurate determination
- B) Unreasonable
- C) Highly technical
- D) Contested without record
  Answer: A
  Explanation: Rule 201 allows notice of indisputable facts.

59. A dying declaration exception applies when the declarant believed death was

- A) Imminent and the statement relates to cause or circumstances of death
- B) Unlikely
- C) Far in the future

- D) Unrelated
  Answer: A
  Explanation: Belief of impending death grounds this hearsay exception.

60. In civil cases, evidence of a person's character is admissible when offered to prove

- A) Character is an essential element of a claim or defense
- B) Propensity to act in conformity
- C) Prior criminal convictions
- D) Gossip
  Answer: A
  Explanation: Character evidence is allowed only when directly in issue.

61. Cross-examination on witness bias is permitted to

- A) Show interest, motive, or bias affecting credibility
- B) Introduce hearsay
- C) Prove the substantive case
- D) Summarize testimony
  Answer: A
  Explanation: Bias evidence is relevant to witness reliability.

62. Lay-witness opinion is allowed on matters

- A) Rationally based on first-hand perception and helpful to the trier of fact
- B) Requiring expert analysis
- C) Purely technical
- D) Speculative
  Answer: A
  Explanation: Lay opinions must stem from direct observation.

63. An expert may testify if

- A) Qualified by knowledge, skill, experience, training, or education and testimony rests on reliable principles
- B) They volunteer
- C) The jury requests
- D) Topics are irrelevant to the case
  Answer: A
  Explanation: Daubert and Rule 702 set expert admissibility standards.

64. Learned treatises may be used to impeach or support expert testimony if

- A) Established as a reliable authority and called to the attention of the expert witness
- B) Introduced by a lay witness
- C) Published recently only
- D) Read to the jury without expert
  Answer: A
  Explanation: Treatises from recognized authorities can aid expert evaluation.

65. Business records exception admits records made

- A) In the regular course of business at or near the time of the event, kept in the regular course
- B) When litigation begins
- C) By a casual observer
- D) Based on memory months later
  Answer: A
  Explanation: Routine entries are presumed reliable absent suspicious facts.

66. Evidence of prior bad acts may be admitted for non-character purposes such as

- A) Motive, opportunity, intent, preparation, plan, knowledge, identity, or absence of mistake
- B) Propensity to commit crime

- C) Sympathy
- D) Default on loan
  Answer: A
  Explanation: Rule 404(b) specifies these permissible reasons.

67. Authentication of real evidence requires a showing that

- A) The evidence is what the proponent claims it is
- B) A witness saw it before
- C) The jury agrees
- D) It is visually distinctive
  Answer: A
  Explanation: Authentication ensures the item's integrity and relevance.

68. Best evidence rule exceptions include duplicates when

- A) No genuine question as to authenticity and fairness would result
- B) Originals lost only by fraud
- C) Secondary evidence is always rejected
- D) Copies are handwritten
  Answer: A
  Explanation: Certified copies or duplicates may suffice absent dispute.

69. The privilege against self-incrimination applies to

- A) Testimony that may incriminate in a criminal case
- B) Civil depositions always
- C) Public records
- D) Physical evidence
  Answer: A
  Explanation: The Fifth Amendment protects testimonial communications.

70. Marital communications privilege covers confidential exchanges

- A) Between spouses during marriage

- B) Observed by a third party
- C) Made in open court
- D) Written letters only
  Answer: A
  Explanation: Spouses cannot be compelled to disclose private communications.

71. Business records admissibility requires testimony or certification attesting to

- A) Source, method of preparation, and that making records was a regular business practice
- B) Non-standard format
- C) Hearsay foundation
- D) Public availability
  Answer: A
  Explanation: Foundation testimony or affidavit establishes the exception.

72. Chain of custody in forensic evidence aims to

- A) Demonstrate integrity by tracking handling from collection to trial
- B) Hide the evidence location
- C) Alter samples
- D) Discard irrelevant items
  Answer: A
  Explanation: Proper chain prevents tampering and ensures reliability.

Real Property (14 Questions)

73. A fee tail estate is one that

- A) Automatically passes to the grantee's descendants lineally
- B) Ends at the grantee's death with no heirs
- C) Lasts for a fixed term

- D) Reverts to the grantor immediately
  Answer: A
  Explanation: Fee tail restricts inheritance to direct descendants.

74. A life estate granted "so long as property used for residential purposes" is

- A) A determinable life estate that ends on condition
- B) A pur autre vie estate
- C) Fee simple absolute
- D) Tenancy at sufferance
  Answer: A
  Explanation: It terminates automatically when the condition fails.

75. If a life tenant commits waste, the remainderman may seek

- A) Injunction and damages for permanent injury
- B) Eviction only
- C) Rent abatement
- D) Lease termination
  Answer: A
  Explanation: Remedies include restoration and compensation.

76. The future interest retained by the grantor after a life estate is

- A) Reversion
- B) Remainder
- C) Fee simple determinable
- D) Fee tail
  Answer: A
  Explanation: Reversion returns the estate to the grantor.

77. A conveyance to "A for life, then to A's children" gives A

- A) A life estate; children a contingent remainder
- B) Fee simple absolute

- C) A leasehold
- D) Fee tail
  Answer: A
  Explanation: A holds a life estate and children take if they exist.

78. An executory interest is a future interest in a transferee that

- A) Cuts short another estate upon a condition
- B) Merely waits to vest after an estate ends
- C) Reverts to the grantor
- D) Applies only in leases
  Answer: A
  Explanation: It divests a prior interest on occurrence of a condition.

79. A tenancy at will terminates upon

- A) Notice by either party or death of landlord or tenant
- B) Fixed term's end
- C) Breach only
- D) Recording a deed
  Answer: A
  Explanation: Either party may end tenancy without a specified term.

80. A tenancy by the entirety is available only to

- A) Married couples with right of survivorship
- B) Co-tenants in common
- C) Life estate holders
- D) Trustees
  Answer: A
  Explanation: Rights reserved for married spouses in certain jurisdictions.

81. Constructive eviction occurs when the landlord's conduct

- A) Renders premises uninhabitable, forcing the tenant to vacate

- B) Raises rent moderately
- C) Fails to repair non-essential items
- D) Refuses to renew the lease
  Answer: A
  Explanation: The tenant must abandon to claim constructive eviction.

82. The Fair Housing Act prohibits discrimination based on

- A) Race, color, religion, sex, familial status, national origin, and disability
- B) Income only
- C) Criminal history
- D) Credit score
  Answer: A
  Explanation: The Act bars these enumerated categories.

83. Delivery of a deed to an escrow agent on condition creates

- A) Equitable title passes when condition is met and escrow closes
- B) Legal title transfers immediately
- C) Fee simple absolute is withheld
- D) Leasehold interest only
  Answer: A
  Explanation: Escrow conditional transfer vests equitable interest on performance.

84. A mortgage creates a

- A) Lien on property securing debt repayment
- B) Fee simple transfer
- C) Life estate
- D) Easement
  Answer: A
  Explanation: A mortgage is a security interest in real property.

85. Judicial foreclosure sale requires notice and

- A) Court order directing sale if the mortgagor defaults
- B) Mortgagee's consent only
- C) Tenant eviction
- D) Quiet title action
  Answer: A
  Explanation: Court supervision ensures fairness in sale.

86. The covenant of quiet enjoyment assures tenants

- A) Possession free from landlord's interference or claims of superior title
- B) Rent abatement only
- C) Subleasing rights
- D) Purchase option
  Answer: A
  Explanation: It protects tenants against wrongful disturbances.

Torts (14 Questions)

87. Assault requires the intent to create

- A) Reasonable apprehension of imminent harmful or offensive contact
- B) Actual contact
- C) Property damage
- D) Fear only if physical injury
  Answer: A
  Explanation: Apprehension of contact suffices; no contact is required.

88. Consent as a defense to battery is ineffective if

- A) Obtained by fraud affecting an essential matter
- B) Express or implied

- C) Given in a medical context only
- D) Non-verbal
  Answer: A
  Explanation: Fraud vitiates consent if it goes to the nature of the act.

89. Strict liability for wild animals applies when the owner

- A) Keeps animals with dangerous propensities in a non-natural environment
- B) Trespasses onto others' land
- C) Bears no responsibility
- D) Domesticates the species
  Answer: A
  Explanation: Inherently dangerous wild animals impose strict liability.

90. Private nuisance occurs when one's use of land

- A) Unreasonably interferes with another's use or enjoyment of their land
- B) Violates zoning only
- C) Causes physical trespass
- D) Is lawful
  Answer: A
  Explanation: Unreasonable interference is the key test.

91. Conversion differs from trespass to chattels because it requires

- A) Serious interference warranting complete title recovery or full-value compensation
- B) Minor damage
- C) Intentional trespass only
- D) No demand for return
  Answer: A
  Explanation: The degree of interference separates conversion from trespass.

92. Negligence per se arises when defendant breaches a statute designed to protect

- A) A specific class of persons from a particular type of harm, causing that harm
- B) General public interest only
- C) Contractual performance
- D) Property rights only
  Answer: A
  Explanation: Violation of a safety statute creates a presumption of breach.

93. Duty to rescue exists when one has

- A) Created the peril or has a special relationship, not merely general public
- B) No relationship
- C) No legal obligation in all jurisdictions
- D) Completed professional training
  Answer: A
  Explanation: Certain relationships impose rescue duties.

94. Good Samaritan statutes protect those who

- A) Voluntarily provide emergency care from ordinary negligence liability
- B) Drive fast
- C) Perform medical procedures for profit
- D) Fail to act
  Answer: A
  Explanation: Statutes encourage aid by reducing liability fears.

95. Res ipsa loquitur permits inference of negligence when

- A) The accident is of a kind that ordinarily does not occur without negligence and the instrumentality was under defendant's control
- B) There are multiple possible causes
- C) Evidence is destroyed intentionally

- D) The plaintiff contributed
  Answer: A
  Explanation: The doctrine shifts the burden to the defendant to explain.

96. The eggshell plaintiff rule holds the defendant liable for

- A) The full extent of the plaintiff's injuries even if more severe than expected
- B) Only foreseeable harm
- C) No unforeseen damages
- D) Damages limited to standard risk
  Answer: A
  Explanation: The defendant takes the plaintiff as found.

97. An employer is vicariously liable for an employee's torts when

- A) The torts occur within the scope of employment
- B) The employee disobeys orders
- C) The employee is off duty
- D) Intentional acts are always excluded
  Answer: A
  Explanation: Scope-of-employment determines liability.

98. Joint and several liability means each defendant

- A) Is independently responsible for the entire judgment amount, subject to contribution among them
- B) Pays an equal share only
- C) Escapes if insolvent
- D) Liability is always limited to fault percentage
  Answer: A
  Explanation: The plaintiff may recover full damages from any liable defendant.

99. Indemnity differs from contribution in that indemnity

- A) Shifts the full loss to one party typically by agreement, whereas contribution apportions among tortfeasors
- B) Is a statutory right only
- C) Applies among joint tortfeasors equally
- D) Is punitive
  Answer: A
  Explanation: Indemnity restores one party to the original position; contribution shares the cost.

100. Punitive damages are awarded to

- A) Punish and deter especially egregious conduct and require clear and convincing evidence of malicious or reckless behavior
- B) Compensate plaintiffs for all losses
- C) Fund public projects
- D) Replace criminal fines
  Answer: A
  Explanation: They deter and punish beyond mere compensation.

Conclusion: Crossing the Finish Line

Well, you made it. You dragged yourself through the preceding chapters, endured the demanding 8-week schedule detailed within, and most importantly, you sat for the bar exam. Whether you walked out feeling elated, defeated, or simply numb and bewildered (a very common reaction, by the way), the fact remains: you crossed the finish line of this particular race. Take a moment – just a brief one, mind you, no need for excessive self-congratulation just yet – to acknowledge the sheer fact of completion. This book laid out a path, a rigorous and structured one, and you chose to follow it. Now, let's briefly look back at that path, give credit where it's due (mostly to your own effort!), and discuss the often surprisingly difficult next phase: life *after* the exam, specifically that dreadful waiting period for results.

Recap of the 8 Week Journey

Cast your mind back eight (or perhaps more, if you factored in the preparatory Part 1) weeks. We started by insisting you **Know Your Enemy** (Chapter 1) – understanding the specific format, scoring, and frequently tested topics of *your* bar exam, rather than operating on rumour or wishful thinking. Then, we focused on **Assembling Your Arsenal** (Chapter 2), emphasizing picking adequate, functional resources and creating a workable study space without getting lost in the foolish pursuit of "perfect" materials or environments.

Chapter 3 demanded **The Starting Line** assessment – using diagnostics not as judgment but as crucial data to honestly identify strengths and weaknesses, leading to setting realistic, **SMART Goals**. And Chapter 4, **Preparing for the Sprint**, addressed the often-neglected but absolutely essential groundwork of clearing your calendar, communicating with your support system, establishing routines for well-being (sleep, nutrition, exercise!), and formulating a proactive **Mental Health Strategy** centered on challenging the irrational beliefs that fuel so much unnecessary suffering during this process.

Then came the core: **Part 2, The 8-Week Daily Breakdown** (Chapters 5-12). Week by week, day by day, the schedule demanded consistent effort, rotating through subjects, and integrating different types of practice:

- Substantive law review (learning the rules).

- Targeted and mixed MBE practice (applying rules in multiple-choice format, building speed).
- Essay writing practice (structuring arguments using IRAC/CRAC, applying rules to facts).
- MPT practice (developing practical lawyering skills under time pressure).
- Crucially, **daily review** of mistakes – because that's where the real learning solidifies.

We moved from **Building the Base** (Week 1) and **Expanding Core Knowledge** (Week 2), through **Integrating Concepts** (Week 3) and the **Midpoint Check-in** (Week 4), into **Ramping Up Practice** (Week 5). Week 6 brought the **Simulation and Refinement** phase with the first full dress rehearsal, followed by Week 7's **Peak Practice & Weak Area Attack**, and finally, Week 8's focus on **Final Polish and Exam Readiness**.

Throughout this schedule, **Part 3: Strategy, Execution, and Beyond** (Chapters 13-16) offered tools to enhance performance. We discussed **Advanced Techniques** for the MBE, essays, and MPTs (Chapter 13), the necessity of truly **Learning from Practice** through effective review and rational adaptation (Chapter 14), navigating **The Final Week** with specific Do's and Don'ts, logistics planning, and mindset management (Chapter 15), and finally, strategies for **Conquering the Exam Days** themselves by managing nerves, timing, and recovery (Chapter 16).

The philosophy underpinning it all was straightforward: **Structure** provides freedom from decision fatigue. **Discipline** is rational self-management in service of your goals. **Active learning** (doing!) beats passive review every time. **Adaptability** means rational adjustment, not catastrophizing minor setbacks. And perhaps most importantly, consistently **challenging your own irrational beliefs** ("I *must* be perfect," "This *should* feel easy," "Failing would be *awful* and *prove* I'm worthless") is key to maintaining motivation and reducing unnecessary emotional distress. It was – and let's not mince words – a demanding, sometimes downright unpleasant, process.

You Did It Acknowledging the Effort

And you did it. You completed the schedule (or your best approximation of it) and you sat for the multi-day examination. Before we talk about the waiting period, it is absolutely essential – rationally essential – that you **acknowledge the effort** you expended, **regardless of how you *feel* you performed or what the eventual outcome might be.**

Many people, especially high-achievers (like most who survive law school), fall into the trap of **conditional self-acceptance**. They only feel good about themselves or value their efforts *if* they achieve a desired outcome, like passing the bar. This is a recipe for misery. It means your self-worth is perpetually held hostage by external results you don't fully control. It also discounts the immense work and sacrifice involved in the *process* itself.

Think about it rationally:

- You dedicated eight weeks (or more) of your life almost exclusively to this goal.
- You likely sacrificed significant social activities, hobbies, relaxation time, and maybe even income.
- You wrestled with complex legal doctrines, forced yourself to practice skills that felt uncomfortable (timed writing, anyone?), and stared down thousands of tricky MBE questions.
- You managed (hopefully!) the accompanying stress, anxiety, fatigue, and self-doubt using the strategies discussed.
- You showed up, day after day, and put in the hours, following a demanding plan.

That effort has value in itself. It demonstrates discipline, resilience, and commitment. It is something *you* accomplished through your own actions. Refusing to acknowledge this effort because you're worried you might not have passed, or because you think you *should* have done more or *should* have felt more confident, is illogical self-deprecation.

Challenge these thoughts:

- "My effort only matters *if* I pass." (Nonsense. The effort demonstrates valuable character traits regardless of the outcome.)
- "I didn't follow the schedule perfectly, so my effort wasn't good enough." (Perfection was never the standard. Consistent, substantial effort *despite* imperfections is what counts.)

- "It felt hard, so I must not have prepared well." (Difficulty is inherent in the task, not necessarily a sign of poor preparation. Tolerating that difficulty *is* part of the accomplishment.)

So, give yourself credit – genuine, unconditional credit – for the sheer work involved in preparing for and sitting for the bar exam according to this (or any other rigorous) plan. You endured the process. That matters.

Life After the Bar Exam Managing the Waiting Period

Ah, the waiting period. Often measured in months, this stretch between finishing the exam and getting results can be a unique form of psychological torture if you let it. Your brain, accustomed to the high-intensity focus of bar prep, might struggle with the sudden lack of structure and the looming uncertainty. This is fertile ground for irrational thinking and misery-inducing behaviors. Let's apply some rational principles here.

Common Irrational Beliefs & Behaviors During the Wait (and how to challenge them):

1. **The Obsessive Debrief/Answer Check:**
    - *Belief:* "I *must* figure out how I did!" "If I can just confirm I got question X right, I'll feel better!" "I *need* to know!"
    - *Behavior:* Frantically searching online forums for discussion of specific questions, trying to reconstruct answers, comparing recollections with peers.
    - *Challenge:* This is utterly futile and harmful. Your memory of specific questions/answers is almost certainly flawed. Online discussions are often filled with misinformation and anxiety-fueled speculation. Knowing the "right" answer to one question tells you absolutely nothing about your overall score, which involves scaling and relative performance. Demanding certainty now, when it's impossible, only creates frustration. **Radical Acceptance:** Accept that you cannot know your score right now. Focusing on it is unproductive torment.
    - *Rational Alternative:* **Strictly avoid** online bar exam forums and post-exam discussions with peers. When the urge arises, acknowledge it ("I

feel the urge to check online") and deliberately redirect your attention to a planned, engaging activity.

2. **Catastrophizing about Perceived Mistakes:**

    - *Belief:* "I totally bombed that one essay/MPT!" "I remember guessing on way too many MBEs!" "Therefore, I definitely failed, and it will be *awful*!"
    - *Behavior:* Ruminating constantly on perceived errors, replaying worst-case scenarios, concluding failure is inevitable.
    - *Challenge:* Your memory of your performance under stress is unreliable. You likely did better than you feel on some parts and perhaps worse on others. One perceived bad essay or a string of MBE guesses does *not* automatically equal failure – partial credit exists, scaling matters, and you might have compensated elsewhere. Awfulizing ("It would be *awful* to fail!") magnifies the negative consequences far beyond reality. Failing is highly inconvenient and disappointing, yes, but unlikely to be the end of your world or career aspirations.
    - *Rational Alternative:* Acknowledge the thought ("I'm worried about that Property essay"). Then challenge the conclusion ("Worrying doesn't change the past. I don't *know* how it was graded. Even if it was weak, I might have done well enough elsewhere. I will deal with the actual results when they arrive. Worrying now changes nothing."). Dispute the awfulizing ("Failing would be bad, but not unbearable. I could retake it.").

3. **Comparing Yourself to Peers:**

    - *Belief:* "Everyone else felt better about it than I did!" "Person X said they found the MBE easy, so I must have done poorly!"
    - *Behavior:* Asking peers how they felt, comparing notes on difficulty, feeling inadequate based on others' (often unreliable) self-assessments.
    - *Challenge:* How others *feel* about the exam is completely irrelevant to your performance. Their subjective impressions are just as likely to be

flawed as yours. Comparing is pointless and usually just makes you feel worse. Focus on your own experience and managing your own thoughts.

- *Rational Alternative:* Refuse to engage in comparisons. If someone asks how you felt, give a vague answer ("It was tough, glad it's over") and change the subject.

4. **Putting Life on Hold / Inability to Tolerate Uncertainty:**

    - *Belief:* "I *can't* relax or enjoy anything until I know my results!" "I *must* know now, I *can't stand* this waiting!" (Low Frustration Tolerance - LFT). "My whole future depends on this!"
    - *Behavior:* Refusing to make plans, apply for jobs, or engage in enjoyable activities. Constant anxiety and irritability due to the inability to tolerate the uncertainty.
    - *Challenge:* You *can* stand the waiting, even though it's unpleasant. You've stood uncomfortable things before. Demanding certainty when none exists is the core problem. Your life does *not* have to stop. While the results are important, they don't define your entire existence or happiness.
    - *Rational Alternative:* **Accept the uncertainty.** Practice telling yourself, "I don't know the results yet, and that's okay for now. I can tolerate this discomfort." **Actively plan and engage in non-bar-related activities.** Reconnect with friends (without talking about the exam!). Restart hobbies. Go on vacation if possible. Apply for jobs (you can always update employers later). Structure your days. Deliberate distraction with pleasant or meaningful activities is a healthy coping mechanism. Challenge LFT: "Waiting is unpleasant, but I *can* stand it."

Scenario: Managing the Wait

- **Anya** spent hours daily on forums, dissecting rumored questions, feeling waves of panic with each post claiming an answer different from what she vaguely remembered. She was miserable and unproductive.
- **Tom**, convinced he failed due to one difficult essay, started preemptively telling family he wouldn't pass and wallowed in self-pity, neglecting job applications.

- **Chloe**, however, made a conscious choice *not* to engage in post-exam discussions. When anxious thoughts about specific questions arose, she acknowledged them ("There's that worry about the Contracts essay") and then actively challenged the catastrophic conclusions ("I don't know how it was graded. Worrying won't change it. Focus on finding a job."). She made plans with friends, started exercising regularly again, and began her job search, accepting the uncertainty but refusing to let it paralyze her. Chloe experienced far less distress during the waiting period. Be like Chloe.

Final Words of Encouragement

You undertook a significant challenge. Following a structured, demanding plan like the one in this book required discipline, focus, and a willingness to confront difficult material and uncomfortable truths about your own thinking patterns. You put in the work.

Now, as you wait for results and look beyond, remember a few things:

- **Unconditional Self-Acceptance:** Your worth as a person is not determined by passing or failing the bar exam. Failing would be a setback, yes, but it doesn't make *you* a failure. Accept yourself, with your strengths and flaws, regardless of the outcome.

- **Focus on Your Locus of Control:** You controlled your preparation efforts. You controlled how you approached the exam days. You can control how you manage the waiting period by challenging irrational thoughts and engaging in healthy behaviors. You cannot control the past performance or the grading process now. Focus your energy where it matters – on your present choices and future actions.

- **Resilience:** You've already demonstrated resilience by getting through law school and this rigorous preparation. Whatever the results, you possess the capacity to handle it and move forward. If you pass, fantastic – begin the next chapter. If you don't, it's deeply disappointing, but you *can* analyze what went wrong (using principles from Chapter 14!), make adjustments, and try again if you choose. It's a hurdle, not necessarily a dead end.

- **Perspective:** In the grand scheme of your life and career, the bar exam is just one step. An important one, to be sure, but not the *only* thing that matters. Maintain perspective.

You took on a tough task and saw it through. Trust the effort you put in, manage your thinking rationally during this uncertain waiting period, and give yourself credit for the hard work accomplished.

Beyond the Scoreboard

The bar exam is over. The intense 8-week schedule is complete. The score, when it comes, is just a number – an important one, no doubt, but still just a number. It doesn't measure your worth, your intelligence, or your potential to be a fine lawyer. What truly matters is the discipline you cultivated, the resilience you showed in facing challenges, and the ability you (hopefully) developed to manage your own thinking, especially when things got tough. Those skills extend far beyond any single exam. Acknowledge the effort, manage the wait rationally by challenging the nonsense your brain might throw at you, and accept yourself unconditionally. You did the work. Now, go live your life while you wait.

References

1. Baer, R.A. (2003) 'Mindfulness training as a clinical intervention: A conceptual and empirical review', *Clinical Psychology: Science and Practice*, 10(2), pp. 125-143.

2. Blackwell, L.S., Trzesniewski, K.H. and Dweck, C.S. (2007) 'Implicit theories of intelligence predict achievement across an adolescent transition: A longitudinal study and an intervention', *Child Development*, 78(1), pp. 246-263.

3. Bjork, R.A. and Bjork, E.L. (2011) 'Making things hard on yourself, but in a good way: Creating desirable difficulties to enhance learning', in Gernsbacher, M.A., Pew, R.W., Hough, L.M. and Pomerantz, J.R. (eds.) *Psychology and the real world: Essays illustrating fundamental contributions to society*. New York: Worth Publishers, pp. 56-64.

4. Britton, B.K. and Tesser, A. (1991) 'Effects of time-management practices on college grades', *Journal of Educational Psychology*, 83(3), pp. 405–410.

5. Brown, P.C., Roediger, H.L. and McDaniel, M.A. (2014) *Make it stick: The science of successful learning*. Cambridge, MA: Harvard University Press.

6. Cassady, J.C. and Johnson, R.E. (2002) 'Cognitive test anxiety and academic performance', *Contemporary Educational Psychology*, 27(2), pp. 270-295.

7. Cepeda, N.J., Pashler, H., Vul, E., Wixted, J.T. and Rohrer, D. (2006) 'Distributed practice in verbal recall tasks: A review and quantitative synthesis', *Psychological Bulletin*, 132(3), pp. 354–380.

8. Chapell, M.S., Blanding, Z.B., Silverstein, M.E., Takahashi, M., Newman, B., Gubi, A. and McCann, N. (2005) 'Test anxiety and academic performance in undergraduate and graduate students', *Journal of Educational Psychology*, 97(2), pp. 268–274.

9. Dunlosky, J., Rawson, K.A., Marsh, E.J., Nathan, M.J. and Willingham, D.T. (2013) 'Improving students' learning with effective learning techniques: Promising directions from cognitive and educational psychology', *Psychological Science in the Public Interest*, 14(1), pp. 4-58.

10. Dweck, C.S. (2006) *Mindset: The new psychology of success*. New York: Random House.

11. Hembree, R. (1988) 'Correlates, causes, effects, and treatment of test anxiety', *Review of Educational Research*, 58(1), pp. 47-77.

12. Karpicke, J.D. and Roediger, H.L. (2008) 'The critical importance of retrieval for learning', *Science*, 319(5865), pp. 966-968.

13. Krieger, L.S. (2005) 'Institutional denial about the dark side of law school, and fresh empirical guidance for constructively navigating the storm', *Villanova Law Review*, 52, p. 87.

14. Macan, T.H., Shahani, C., Dipboye, R.L. and Phillips, A.P. (1990) 'College students' time management: Correlations with academic performance and stress', *Journal of Educational Psychology*, 82(4), pp. 760–768.

15. Paas, F., Renkl, A. and Sweller, J. (2003) 'Cognitive load theory and instructional design: Recent developments', *Educational Psychologist*, 38(1), pp. 1-4.

16. Pintrich, P.R. (2004) 'A conceptual framework for assessing motivation and self-regulated learning in college students', *Educational Psychology Review*, 16(4), pp. 385-407.

17. Putwain, D.W. (2007) 'Test anxiety in UK schoolchildren: Prevalence and demographic patterns', *British Journal of Educational Psychology*, 77(3), pp. 579-593.

18. Rasch, B. and Born, J. (2013) 'About sleep's role in memory', *Physiological Reviews*, 93(2), pp. 681-766.

19. Roediger, H.L. and Karpicke, J.D. (2006) 'Test-enhanced learning: Taking memory tests improves long-term retention', *Psychological Science*, 17(3), pp. 249-255.

20. Rohrer, D. and Pashler, H. (2007) 'Increasing retention without increasing study time', *Current Directions in Psychological Science*, 16(4), pp. 183-186.

21. Ryan, C.J. and Muller, D.T. (2023) 'The Secret Sauce: Examining Law Schools that Overperform on the Bar Exam', *Indiana Law Journal*, 98(Supplement), pp. 65-118.

22. Shapiro, S.L., Schwartz, G.E. and Bonner, G. (1998) 'Effects of mindfulness-based stress reduction on medical and premedical students', *Journal of Behavioral Medicine*, 21(6), pp. 581-599.

23. Sheldon, K.M. and Krieger, L.S. (2007) 'Understanding the negative effects of legal education on law students: A longitudinal test of self-determination theory', *Personality and Social Psychology Bulletin*, 33(6), pp. 883-897.

24. Stickgold, R. (2005) 'Sleep-dependent memory consolidation', *Nature*, 437(7063), pp. 1272-1278.

25. Sweller, J. (1988) 'Cognitive load during problem solving: Effects on learning', *Cognitive Science*, 12(2), pp. 257-285.

26. Sweller, J., van Merriënboer, J.J.G. and Paas, F. (1998) 'Cognitive architecture and instructional design', *Educational Psychology Review*, 10(3), pp. 251-296.

27. Trujillo, L.A. (2007) 'The Relationship Between Law School and the Bar Exam: A Look at Assessment and Student Success', *University of Colorado Law Review*, 78(1), pp. 69-126.

28. Wightman, L.F. (1998) *LSAC national longitudinal bar passage study*. LSAC Research Report Series. Newtown, PA: Law School Admission Council.

29. Yeager, D.S. and Dweck, C.S. (2012) 'Mindsets that promote resilience: When students believe that personal characteristics can be developed', *Educational Psychologist*, 47(4), pp. 302-314.

30. Zeidner, M. (1998) *Test anxiety: The state of the art*. New York: Plenum Press.

31. Zimmerman, B.J. (2002) 'Becoming a self-regulated learner: An overview', *Theory Into Practice*, 41(2), pp. 64-70.

Made in United States
Orlando, FL
05 November 2026

90230141R00111